paradoxes of emotion
and fiction

robert j yanal

paradoxes of emotion
and fiction

THE PENNSYLVANIA STATE UNIVERSITY PRESS   UNIVERSITY PARK, PENNSYLVANIA

Library of Congress Cataloging-in-Publication Data

Yanal, Robert J.
   Paradoxes of emotion and fiction / Robert J. Yanal.
      p.   cm.
   Includes bibliographical references and index.
   ISBN 0-271-01893-3 (cloth : alk. paper)
   ISBN 0-271-01894-1 (pbk. : alk. paper)
   1. Emotions (Philosophy)   2. Fiction.   I. Title.
   B105.E46 Y37   1999
   128'.37—ddc21   98-43075
                                                CIP

It is the policy of The Pennsylvania State University Press to use acid-free paper for the first printing of all clothbound books. Publications on uncoated stock satisfy the minimum requirements of American National Standard for Information Sciences—Permanence of Paper for Printed Library Materials, ANSI Z39.48-1992.

to larry spencer

contents

preface and acknowledgments

A certain problem, barely noticed previously, was raised in an Aristotelian Society symposium between Colin Radford and Michael Weston in 1975. This problem turned out to be what I call the paradox of emotion and fiction. It provoked a surprisingly large commentary, beginning mainly with critical responses to Radford, which themselves developed a variety of different solutions to the paradox. Another and more durable strand of the literature on the paradox began with Kendall Walton's paper in the 1978 *Journal of Philosophy*, "Fearing Fictions," the theory in which was further developed in his highly regarded book *Mimesis as Make-Believe* (Harvard University Press, 1990) and the criticisms and responses to Walton's theory.

Indeed, this puzzle and its literature occupies a good part of the history of recent aesthetics, and commentary continues to spew forth even as I write. The paradox of emotion and fiction is one of the few problematics of recent aesthetics that can be cast into competing schools of thought, putting it, for better or worse, on the same footing as solutions to the mind-body problem, the free-will question, and other mainstream philosophical issues.

One goal of this book is to classify and assess these solutions. Another is to put forward and defend a version of a solution called "thought theory" against its main competitor, Walton's theory of make-believe. Two less-traveled but equally interesting paradoxes are also addressed, the paradox of suspense and the paradox of tragedy.

It was Walton's reading of "Fearing Fictions" at Wayne State University just before it appeared in the *Journal of Philosophy* that stimulated my thinking on the problem. I might mark my conversion against Walton's view as a meta-reaction to my emotions while viewing a two-character movie, *'Night Mother*, based on Marsha Norman's Pulitzer Prize-winning play starring Anne Bancroft as a dependent mother and Sissy Spacek as her epileptic daughter. Spacek's character has decided that her life as an epileptic is without happiness or hope and that she will commit suicide. Through the night in which the story takes place, Bancroft tries to talk Spacek out of killing herself while Spacek lucidly and doggedly argues her case. As the final gun shot sounds behind a closed door, I felt enormous sadness and the thought came to me (as it did to Mia Farrow's Rosemary coming briefly to consciousness during her devilish intercourse): "This is real." When Rosemary uttered this cry, she meant "as opposed to a dream," but I meant "as opposed to quasi-sadness." I groped toward a theory that did not yield Walton's result, and found the basis for one in Peter Lamarque's defense of thought theory in his 1981 *British Journal of Aesthetics* essay, "How Can We Fear and Pity Fictions?"

I am grateful to Peter Lamarque and an anonymous referee, who made helpful and supportive suggestions on earlier drafts of the manuscript. I'm appreciative also of the work of folks at Penn State Press, especially Sandy Thatcher, the Press's editor, who shepherded the manuscript through reviews to acceptance, and Patty Mitchell, copyeditor, who fine-tuned the details. I'd like to acknowledge members of my 1994 and 1998 graduate seminars on the paradoxes: Ann Kennedy, Jim Tierney, Sam Von Mizener, Sadegh Emari, Erik Roys, Steve Patterson, Carrie Shea, Bill Warda, Mark Wenzel, Ron Warren, and especially Ed Gron, Mike McFerren, and Mark Huston for their questions and comments.

I have in Chapter 4 (on Kendall Walton) borrowed from my article "The Paradox of Emotion and Fiction," *Pacific Philosophical Quarterly* 75 (1994): 54–75; and in Chapter 9 (on the paradox of tragedy) from two discussion notes, "Hume and Others on the Paradox of Tragedy," *Journal of Aesthetics and Art Criticism* 49 (1991): 75–76; and "Still Unconverted: A Reply to Neill," *Journal of Aesthetics and Art Criticism* 50 (1992): 324–26. Chapter 8 (on the paradox of suspense) appeared in an earlier version in the *British Journal of Aesthetics* 36 (1996): 146–58.

the paradox
of emotion
and fiction

There is a famous sequence in Alfred Hitchcock's 1959 film, *North by Northwest*, in which Roger Thornhill, played by Cary Grant, is pursued and very nearly killed by a flying crop-dusting plane. Thornhill has been given directions to meet the mysterious "Mr. Kaplan." He is to take a certain bus out of Chicago and get off at "Prairie Stop–Highway 41," which turns out to be nothing more than a country road in the middle of some fields. After some long moments, a car pulls up and drops off a man who, it turns out, is not "Mr. Kaplan" but just a local farmer waiting for the next bus. A crop duster plane is seen in the distance. As his bus pulls up the farmer says to Thornhill, "That's funny. That plane's dusting crops where there ain't no crops."

The bus pulls away and Thornhill is left standing on the road alone. The plane seems to be flying closer to him and, with mounting alarm, he realizes that the plane is *diving* at him—and not only diving but *shooting* at him. Thornhill hits the ground as the plane buzzes just over his head, spraying bullets. He gets up, but again the plane fires just over his head, narrowly missing him. Thornhill runs into a nearby field to take cover in a patch of dried corn stalks. But now the plane roars over the corn stalks spraying white dusty pesticide. Choking, he is forced out into the open and begins to run toward the road. Just then, he spies a truck and rushes out to stop it. The truck very nearly runs him over as it lurches to a stop. The crop duster, however, has followed Thornhill but now cannot avoid crashing into the truck that happens to be carrying gasoline. Thornhill and the truck driver escape, just before both plane and truck explode into flames.

Paradox and Fiction

This is a book about how emotions toward fiction are paradoxical, and how something called "thought theory" solves the paradox. But where is the paradox? Isn't having a good cry over a sad movie a simple fact of life? On the surface it is, but we'll find on probing deeper that there are good reasons to wonder how the good cry is even possible.

What, to begin with, is a paradox? A paradox is a set of apparent truths that are, taken together, contradictory. A paradox is, in other words, a state of affairs that appears impossible yet true. Contradictions, of course, can't be true (they're impossible, false in all possible worlds). But certain contradictory states of affairs can *seem* true, and this is what gives piquancy to a paradox. The liar paradox, which is of ancient origin, has it that a certain Cretan says, "I am now telling a lie." Is what he says true or false? It seems both, for if he speaks truly, he is lying and so what he says is false; yet if false, he is not lying, hence what he says is true; but if true, he is lying . . . and so on.

A paradox that troubled Frege and Russell,[1] and which called into question the nature of sets, is the barber of Seville, who shaves everyone in Seville who does not shave himself. But now it seems that the barber both shaves and does not shave himself: if he does not shave himself then

---

1. Russell communicated the barber paradox in a 1902 letter to Gottlob Frege. In his answer, Frege confirmed that the discovery of the paradox had shaken the foundation of the system of logic on which he intended to build arithmetic. Both letters are included in John van Heijenoort, ed., *From Frege to Gödel: A Source Book in Mathematical Logic, 1879–1931* (Cambridge, Mass.: Harvard University Press, 1967).

he must shave himself; but if he shaves himself then he does not shave himself. We know there can't *really* be a contradiction—what the Cretan says can't, in the end, really be both true and false, Russell's barber can't in the final analysis both shave and not shave himself—but there seems to be one, and the trick is to find a means to dissolve the contradiction. Often, the attempt to dissolve a paradox brings a new idea into play, as when Russell offered type theory as a solution to the barber paradox, and Tarski distinguished between languages and metalanguages to solve the liar.[2] It is hoped that a solution to the paradox of emotion and fiction will shed some light both on our emotional responses to fiction and on the nature of emotion itself.

How do our emotional reactions to fiction end up in paradox? Consider first the apparent fact of these emotions. Audience members watching *North by Northwest* are already concerned for Roger Thornhill. After all, Thornhill, even before the episode on Highway 41, has been kidnapped and questioned as if he were a "Mr. Kaplan." He'd had whiskey poured down his throat and been put behind the wheel of a car which was sent down a dangerous mountain road; he'd been photographed holding a UN delegate who has just been stabbed; and, in fleeing the police, he had been seduced and then jilted by Eve Kendall (Eva Marie Saint). Now, there he is, standing on a nearly deserted rural highway. The farmer's remark about the crop duster brings on yet more feelings of unease. Why is a plane flying over these fields if there are no crops to be dusted? Audience members are startled, then horrified when the plane shoots at Thornhill. They fear for Thornhill's life as he ducks the plane. They are aghast at the fiery crash of plane into gasoline truck, though they are relieved when Thornhill jumps into a pickup truck and escapes. The audience, in other words, experiences a range of emotions toward Roger Thornhill—who is a fictional character.

This phenomenon is, of course, not unique to *North by Northwest* or to film in general. We often have feelings for fictional characters in novels, plays, films, opera, even painting. In Laura Esquivel's *Like Water for Chocolate*, we hate Mama Elena for refusing to allow her daughter Tita to marry the man she loves, forcing her to remain single so that Tita can take

2. Bertrand Russell, "Mathematical Logic as Based on the Theory of Types," first published in 1908, reprinted in a collection of Russell's essays, *Logic and Knowledge: Essays 1901–1950*, edited by Robert Charles Marsh (New York: Macmillan, 1956). For Alfred Tarski's solution to the liar paradox, see his paper, "The Concept of Truth in Formalized Languages," in the collection of Tarski's essays, *Logic, Semantics, Metamathematics: Papers from 1923 to 1938*, translated by J. H. Woodger (Oxford: Clarendon Press, 1956).

care of Mama Elena in her old age. We become impatient and a bit sad as Marty and Angie sit around asking each other, "So what do you feel like doing tonight?" in Paddy Chayefsky's *Marty*. We fall just a little bit in love with Audrey Hepburn's Princess Anne in William Wyler's *Roman Holiday*. We admire the Marshallin's grace and nobility and sympathize with her heartbreak as she encourages her young lover Octavian to marry Sophie in the concluding Act 3 trio of Richard Strauss's *Der Rosenkavalier*—some of the most beautiful music ever written—for we hope that Octavian and Sophie might be happy, but we know that the Marshallin is resigned to a socially acceptable but loveless marriage.

However, the paradox does not arise simply because people on occasion have emotions toward what in fact are fictional characters. One could, wrongly and implausibly but possibly, take Roger Thornhill to be a real person (and Hitchcock's film to be accurate biography or docudrama); and under these circumstances feeling anxiety over Roger Thornhill's cornfield predicament would not verge toward paradox. While reading Tolstoy's *War and Peace*, a patriotic Russian reader, who is jubilant over Napoleon's defeat at the hands of the Moscow winter, and who takes Napoleon and his defeat to be historical, is jubilant that his (real) ancestors (really) defeated the (real) Napoleon, and there is no paradox lurking in that.

Imagine a catastrophe (collision with an asteroid, say) that nearly destroys humanity. The few survivors lose the art of literacy but over generations regain it and attempt to reconnect with the civilization that has been destroyed. They chance upon Jane Austen's *Emma*, title page missing, which they (mistakenly) take to be a biography of a certain Emma Woodhouse who is handsome, clever, and rich. This audience does not take Emma Woodhouse to be a fiction, and any emotions they have toward her would not be paradoxical. Conversely, we can imagine the same catastrophe with the opposite result: the survivors come across, say, Thomas Keneally's book, *Schindler's List*, which they take to be fictional (perhaps it strikes them as improbable and hence invented). For that audience, the dismay they might feel when reading about the plight of the Polish Jews or the grudging admiration they accord Oskar Schindler would be paradoxical, for these would be emotions directed toward what this audience, wrongly as it happens, takes to be fictions.

What makes the difference between the prosaic and the paradoxical is therefore not quite having emotions toward fiction (though I will sometimes for brevity's sake put it that way), but more precisely having emotions toward *what one takes to be a fiction*. What is it to take something to be a fiction? Richard Moran, in a generally insightful paper, thinks that emotions toward what one takes to be fictional are not especially aberrant since we often experience emotions—anticipation, remorse—toward what is to come or what is past, in any case toward what is absent from present sensory awareness. For example,

> the person who says that it still makes her shudder just to think about her driving accident, or her first date, is exhibiting one of the paradigms of emotional response, not an exception to the norm. Now admittedly these will be responses to some real event, even if in the past. Nonetheless, I think the comparison with the case of fiction is still appropriate here since if shuddering in a movie theater is paradoxical, then so ought to be shuddering sitting safely at home years after one's experience.[3]

But to respond emotionally to what one takes to be fictional is not merely to respond to what happens to be absent to one's present consciousness. I may pity a man condemned to death though I am not presently in sensory contact with him. Such a man may have been already executed; or he may be incarcerated across the continent, his case known to me only though the newspapers; or he may be facing execution sometime in the future. It is the thought that he is suffering—a point I will return to with some force later—that brings on my pity. Still, there would appear to be a great difference between feeling pity for someone whom one has never met and feeling pity for a fictional character in a novel who has been condemned to death. It is only real people who really suffer (or who really have suffered, or who really will suffer).

What, then, is it to take someone (or something) to be fictional? On the simplest possible characterization: to take something to be fictional is to believe (or assume) that it doesn't exist. But this characterization is *too* simple, for past and future things (my birth, my death) don't exist *now*, though that alone does not deem them to be fictional events. If we take *Anna Karenina* to be fictional, we believe that Tolstoy's novel in which she appears is not disguised biography. We take it that there is no real person about whom Tolstoy wrote—that *Anna Karenina* is not a *roman à clef*. Nor do we take Tolstoy's novel as the sort of narrative that could turn out

---

3. Richard Moran, "The Expression of Feeling in Imagination," *Philosophical Review* 103 (1994): 78.

to be true of someone unknown to Tolstoy—accidental biography, so to speak—if an actual woman were to be truly, though improbably, describable as Tolstoy's tragic heroine. To take something to be fictional, on the next simplest characterization, is to take it never to exist at any time.

This latter characterization, though, is controverted by some philosophical theories which have it that what we ordinarily call "fictional characters" do in some attenuated sense exist. For example, according to Noël Carroll, "The name 'Dracula' refers to its sense, the congeries of properties attributed to the vampire in the novel," properties such as *being impure* and *being fearsome*.[4] So it would not do to say that Carroll, who surely takes Dracula to be fictional, thereby takes Dracula to fail *absolutely* to exist, since for Carroll Dracula exists as a congeries of properties. One might well have metaphysical scruples against the notion that there could be a diune congeries of pure properties, *impurity and fearsomeness*, without there being a particular that instantiates such properties, though if one acknowledges the existence of properties it seems a short step to acknowledging combinations of properties (still, what holds them "together"?). I find little attraction in Carroll's theory, but it is a theory according to which fictional entities have a sort of existence—they do not, that is, fail to exist entirely.

We cannot then define "taking X to be a fiction" as "taking X *entirely* to fail to exist," for some philosopher-reader may not quite do that. Still, not even the philosopher-reader expects to encounter what he takes to be a fiction in space and time as a particular. Dracula may be a congeries of properties; but what he is *not* is a vampire that you could have physically encountered as a material particular in nineteenth-century England. Put another way, fictional entities don't exist in the way that they purport to exist, which is as particulars in the world we readers and viewers now occupy, particulars that are affected (who have experiences and feelings)

---

4. Noël Carroll, *The Philosophy of Horror, or Paradoxes of the Heart* (New York: Routledge, 1990), 86. Carroll's view is an expansion of an earlier view by Peter Lamarque, borrowing on a still earlier theory by Gottlob Frege, according to which works of fiction are a species of indirect discourse whose names denote not their in-the-world referent (if any) but their sense. On Frege's original understanding, in the direct context, "Dracula is Transylvanian," the name "Dracula" refers to its in-the-world referent, which is nothing at all (for there is no Dracula). In the indirect context, "Yanal said that Dracula is Transylvanian," the name "Dracula" refers to its sense. Lamarque amends Frege slightly, taking a work of fiction to be a species of indirect context. In effect, we are to understand "Dracula is Transylvanian" to be shorthand for "Bram Stoker narrates that Dracula is Transylvanian," thus generating the indirect context. Carroll in turn reifies Lamarque's suggestion, turning senses into congeries of properties. See Peter Lamarque, "Fictional Characters," in his book of essays *Fictional Points of View* (Ithaca: Cornell University Press, 1996), 33ff.

and who can affect other particulars. So to take something to be a fiction is to believe (or assume) that that something is not, and never has been nor ever will be, an experiential spatio-temporal particular in the actual world. This leaves it open that someone could take X to be a fiction and yet X exists as an abstract object; though the point for emotional response is that abstractions can neither hurt you nor can they suffer or perform heroic deeds, so that it would seem that abstractions won't generate emotion.

What is taken to be a fiction may, of course, vary from person to person. The five-year-old takes Santa Claus to be real (he believes Santa Claus actually comes down his chimney); the six-year-old takes him to be a fiction. But commixtures of fact and fiction are not always the result of childish confusion. The historian Arnold Toynbee wrote, "It has been said of the *Iliad* that anyone who starts reading it as history will find that it is full of fiction but, equally, anyone who starts reading it as fiction will find that it is full of history."[5] It may be that Achilles was a real personage of Agamemnon's army, and that Homer wrote about him. Still, most modern readers take Achilles to be a fiction even though they may take the war with Troy to be historical. E. L. Doctorow's work *Ragtime* mingles (what I take to be) real people (Evelyn Nesbit, Harry K. Thaw, Stanford White, Booker T. Washington, Harry Houdini) with (what I take to be) fictional characters (Younger Brother, Father, Sarah, Mother, Coalhouse Walker, etc.). Readers Albert and Betty may both feel fierce anger at the injustice done to Coalhouse Walker (local volunteer firemen, enraged that a black man would own a Model T, pile horse manure on its front seat), but Albert takes him and the Model T insult to be fictional, while Betty takes him to be real and the incident true. Only Albert's anger leans toward paradox.

I should emphasize that for purposes of generating paradox, it doesn't matter if one is *correct* in what one takes to be a fiction. Albert may take Stanford White to be a fiction, perhaps because Albert has never heard of him; Betty takes Stanford White to be a real person, perhaps because she has heard of him; the author E. L. Doctorow may assert that he intended "Stanford White" to refer to the historical architect and philanderer, and so relative to the author's intent, Albert is wrong. What matters is that Albert takes Stanford White to be a fiction and that any emotions Albert has toward that "character" verge toward paradox.

---

5. Quoted by Edmund Fuller, in his "Editor's Note" to his abridgment of *Bulfinch's Mythology* (New York: Dell Publishing, 1959), 5. I am unable to locate the original source.

We primarily engage our emotions with fictions in the course of narratives—plays, ballads, novels, stories told aloud, films, opera, to some extent painting. And here I pause to introduce a term. Given the various senses employed to engage ourselves with the narrative—we say we *saw* the play, *heard* the ballad, *viewed* the film—there will occasionally be a need for a genus word, and I'll then speak of an audience as *receiving* the narrative, and sometimes of an audience themselves as *receivers*. It is common to speak of certain narratives as works of fiction, though my principal concern here is not the objective issue of when a certain narrative is a work of fiction and when not, but the subjective issue of when someone takes a certain narrative to be about fictions. For most of us, *Emma* is a work of fiction because we take all of its characters to be fictions; for the survivors of the asteroid collision, *Emma* is not a work of fiction, and it matters not at all for the purposes of paradox that these survivors are objectively wrong. What I'll mean, then, by "a work of fiction" (to the extent I'll make use of the concept) is the relativized "work of fiction for a certain class of receivers." A class of receivers takes something to be a work of fiction when they take most of its characters to be fictions. Still, the starting point for paradox is the case of a receiver who takes a character to be a fiction and nonetheless fears or pities or admires that character.

Where, though, is the paradox? In a pair of papers that begins recent discussions of this problem, Colin Radford and Michael Weston ask, How can we pity Anna Karenina when we take her to be a fiction, given that by taking her to be a fiction we acknowledge that there isn't someone who really suffers or commits suicide?[6] Yet we pity Anna Karenina, feel anxious over Roger Thornhill's plight, are impatient over Marty's lack of direction, hate Mama Elena for her extravagantly selfish demands, and feel admiration for the Marschallin's resignation, though we take each of these to be a fiction. It is apparently true that

1. Some people (we'll call them emoters) on occasion experience emotions toward characters or situations they take to be fictions.

I shall often put the point more briefly: emoters sometimes experience emotions toward fictions.

---

6. Colin Radford, in symposium with Michael Weston, "How Can We Be Moved By the Fate of Anna Karenina?," *Proceedings of the Aristotelian Society*, supp. vol. 49 (1975).

Emotion and Belief

Proposition 1, by itself of course, isn't paradoxical (it isn't self-contradictory, self-evidently odd, not even by itself puzzling). More must be added to get to paradox. According to Colin Radford, "It would seem then that I can only be moved by someone's plight if I believe that something terrible has happened to him. If I do not believe that he has not and is not suffering or whatever, I cannot grieve or be moved to tears."[7] But Radford is not entirely on point here. The emoter in a plain sense believes that a character named Roger Thornhill is in danger from a plane that is shooting at him. What he doesn't believe is that Roger Thornhill exists (for he takes him, correctly as it happens, to be a fiction). This begins to be brought out by Kendall Walton, who offers an example that has become well known in the literature on this problem.

> Charles is watching a horror movie about a terrible green slime. He cringes in his seat as the slime oozes slowly but relentlessly over the earth destroying everything in its path. . . . The slime, picking up speed, oozes on a new course straight toward the viewers. Charles emits a shriek and clutches desperately at his chair. Afterwards, still shaken, he confesses that he was 'terrified' of the slime.
>
> *Was* he terrified of it? I think not.[8]

Commenting on this case, Walton says, "It would not be far wrong to argue simply as follows: to fear something is in part to think oneself endangered by it. Charles does not think he is endangered by the slime. So he does not fear it." This is not a peculiarity of *fear* toward fictional characters.

> We should be wary of the idea that people literally pity Willy Loman or grieve for Anna Karenina or admire Superman while being fully aware that these characters and their sufferings or exploits are purely fictitious. It is not implausible that pity involves a belief (or judgment, or attitude) that what one pities actually suffers misfortune, and admiration a belief that the

---

7. Radford, "How Can We Be Moved?," 68.
8. Kendall Walton, *Mimesis as Make-Believe* (Cambridge: Harvard University Press, 1990), 196. The example originates in an earlier paper by Walton, "Fearing Fictions," *Journal of Philosophy*, 75 (1978): 5–27.

admired object is admirable, but the normal appreciator does not think it is actually the case that Willy suffers or that Superman is admirable.[9]

Clearly, Radford and Walton think it necessary to have certain beliefs in order to have emotions, beliefs, it appears, that the emoter toward fictions lacks. However, they do not specify the *general* form of the belief necessary. We must believe that Willie Loman suffers or that Superman is admirable, yes, but what is the broader principle at issue? We can grope toward it by starting with the reasonable assumption that some set of features of the world will tend to trigger in the typical observer a certain emotion, while another set of features will tend to trigger another emotion. A person suffering is among the set of features that will tend to trigger pity in the typical observer, and a person in extreme danger is among the set of features that will tend to trigger anxiety. Clearly, the set of features will vary from emotion to emotion. That is, the features that tend to trigger anxiety will be quite different (probably entirely different) from the features that tend to trigger admiration.

What triggers which emotion in any particular individual is also variable, though we expect that humans will on the whole exhibit predictable and not anomalous emotional response. Suffering, for example, will tend to arouse pity not joy in the typical observer (that's what makes him typical). So, as a general rule, we can state that there is a constellation of features for each emotion such that when some features of this constellation are instantiated in the world and observed by a person, that person will typically experience that emotion (though the paradox of emotion and fiction can be aroused by atypical emotional responses: someone who feels delight at Anna Karenina's plight is still feeling emotion toward what he takes to be fictional). We'll call such a constellation "emotion-inducing properties." The general principle that Radford and Walton hint at can be stated this way:

2. Any person experiences an emotion only if he believes that the object of his emotion both exists and exhibits at least some of the emotion inducing properties specific to that emotion.

The apparent truth of proposition 2 can be explained at least by this: people do not usually have emotions in the absence of any perceived emotion-inducing properties. People do not have emotions out of the clear blue sky or for no reason—or if they do, the very absence of apparent cause itself requires special explanation (unconscious beliefs, hallucination, etc.). People do not, for example, suddenly experience pity for someone without believing them to have some pity-inducing property. Or worse, they do not stare off into space at nothing and say, "I pity that poor man who has lost his dog," when plainly there is no poor man, no lost dog, indeed, nothing to pity at all. To the prospective pitier, someone should at the minimum exist but also appear impoverished or ill, or seem mad or in pain, or the like. Further, if the observer thinks someone is shamming pain—if the observer does not believe there is pain—he will not experience pity (though he might experience contempt or anger).

And now to get to our experience of fiction. Emoters, according to Radford and Walton, do not believe that something terrible has happened to Anna Karenina, do not believe that Willy Loman suffers, and so on. In general, then:

3. No emoter who takes the object of his emotion to be fiction believes that the object of his emotion exists and exhibits any emotion inducing properties.

Proposition 3 seems to be not just true but *analytically* true: if I take something to be a fiction, then I take it that it isn't an experiencing or causally efficacious spatio-temporal particular, hence something that has no real emotion-inducing properties.

We have come to paradox. I'll repeat the propositions here for the reader's convenience.

The Paradox Set
1. Some people (we'll call them emoters) on occasion experience emotions toward characters or situations they take to be fictions.
2. Any person experiences an emotion only if he believes that the object of his emotion both exists and exhibits at least some of the emotion inducing properties specific to that emotion.
3. No emoter who takes the object of his emotion to be fiction believes that the object of his emotion exists and exhibits any emotion inducing properties.

Propositions 2 and 3 logically imply that emotion toward fiction is an impossibility, and yet proposition 1 claims emotions toward fiction to be an occasional occurrence. We thus have yet cannot have emotions toward fiction.

Solving the Paradox

A paradox is a set of contradictory apparent truths. Not all propositions that make up any paradox set can *actually* be true, for contradictions cannot be true. At least one proposition from a paradox set must be in reality false even if it appears true. The centerpiece of a solution to a paradox is the proposition it argues to be the falsehood. Indeed, it is possible to classify any solution to the paradox according to which proposition of the paradox set it singles out as the offending falsehood.

Most solutions, strangely enough, deny the first proposition of the paradox set. One class of solutions (which I call Factualism) asserts that emoters do not experience emotions toward what they take to be fictions but rather toward certain actualities called to mind by the fictions. On one Factualist solution, an emoter does not pity Anna Karenina but rather people like her or people in her straits. This trades fiction for fact, and no one finds anything paradoxical about feeling emotion toward fact. Kendall Walton's influential theory also denies the first proposition, insisting that emoters do not really experience emotions toward what they take to be fictions but rather the more attenuated "quasi-emotions." And quasi-emotions are not ruled by the psychological law stated in proposition 3; hence, there is no inconsistency between feeling quasi-emotions and failing to have the kinds of beliefs that proposition 3 seems to require.

Another class of solutions denies the second proposition. Colin Radford argues that any *rational* person experiences an emotion only if he believes that the object of his emotion exists and has the relevant emotion-inducing properties, a view that is in concord with the other propositions of the paradox set. But peace here comes at a price: emoters toward fiction are behaving irrationally. Thought theory, the view I'll defend, also denies the second proposition, arguing that belief is not necessary for emotion. Thought (under certain circumstances) without belief can stimulate emotion—in John Morreall's pithy characterization: "What is important to our feeling emotion toward a situation is not whether we believe that the situation exists, but rather how vividly and engagingly that situation is presented to our consciousness, in either perception, memory, or imagination."[10] Samuel Taylor Coleridge is the progenitor of thought theory; it receives contemporary formulations in some writings by Roger Scruton, Peter Lamarque, and Susan Feagin, among others. This book propounds and defends a version of thought theory in Chapter 7. The most viable solutions to the paradox on the contemporary scene are Walton's theory of quasi-emotions and thought theory. I'll thus spend considerable space attacking the former and defending the latter.

A Prehistory of the Paradox

There are two golden ages in aesthetics: Ancient Greece and the Century of Taste (George Dickie's name for the eighteenth century). Interestingly, at no time in either age is the paradox recognized, with one exception. The paradox of emotion and fiction is, then, *not* one of the perennial problems of philosophy "as old as Plato."

The audience who emoted toward the rhapsodes reciting Homer (and whose emotional responses were to send up red flags for Plato) might have puzzled ancient writers as much as they did Radford and Weston. But no such puzzle arises. The explanation consists, I think, of this: it takes the recognition that some narratives are about fictional nonentities. To describe, let alone solve, the paradox of emotion and fiction, a theory of "mimetic" art must recognize (or posit) that the audience for Homer acknowledges that there is no Achilles who has lost his best friend Patroclus, hence no one to pity for his painful grief. And for different reasons, neither Plato nor Aristotle incorporates recognition of fictionality in their theories of mimetic art.

In his well-known trichotomy in Book X of the *Republic*, Plato tells us that god creates the form or original of a bed, a carpenter makes a particular bed by imitating that which god made, and the mimetic artist imitates the mere appearance of that which the carpenter made.[11] Mimetic artworks are thus on a par with shadows and mirror images. Their claim to truth is limited (Plato tells us they are "an indistinct expression of truth"), though they contain a certain deceptive power, the mimetic artist

10. John Morreall, "Enjoying Negative Emotions in Fictions," *Philosophy and Literature* 9 (1985): 100.

11. The translation of Plato's *Republic* used is by Benjamin Jowett, in *The Dialogues of Plato*, 4th ed. (Oxford: Clarendon Press, 1953).

being a kind of "wizard" who excels at making appearance look real. The good painter "may deceive children or simple persons when he shows them his picture of a carpenter from a distance, and they will fancy that they are looking at a real carpenter"—though Plato thinks when it comes to art, Homer especially, all of us become a bit simple, "such is the sweet influence which melody and rhythm by nature have." The "calculating and rational principle in the soul" must come to our rescue, to distinguish appearance from reality. The stick that appears to be bent in the water is corrected by reason to be in truth straight. It is reason's correcting power that is stifled by powerful art. When Homer "represents some hero who is drawling out his sorrows in a long oration, or singing, and smiting his breast—the best of us . . . delight in giving way to sympathy, and are in raptures at the excellence of the poet who stirs our feelings most." Poetic narration "feeds and waters the passions instead of drying them up." Poetry is unhealthy and deceptive but not paradoxical. It presents an unreality, though such is its power that its audience does not acknowledge the unreality, hence responds to poetical imitations as if to real things. But it is important to note that for Plato, the audience to Homer does not wrongly take *fiction* for reality. Such an audience wrongly takes *appearance* for reality, and while appearance isn't quite reality, it isn't exactly fictional either. The mistake such an audience makes is not the same as—is less than—the mistake we would make were we to take King Lear to be a real person. It is more like the mistake someone might make in taking a mirror image to be real.

And there is another reason why Plato could not see a paradox of emotion toward fiction. What Plato seems to have assumed is just as there must be a form of a bed for the carpenter to imitate, so there must be a particular bed for the artist to paint. The mimetic artist cannot make anything up in Plato's view, for he is forever beholden to material particulars, else he would have nothing whose appearance he could imitate. Homer, too, could not have composed the *Iliad* without benefit of an actual war with Troy, for while Agamemnon as general of the Achians is (presumably) imitating the form of leadership (i.e., trying his best to be a good general), Homer is merely imitating what Agamemnon does, both mistakes (bad generalship) and good moves, with Plato's worry being that Homer qua mimetic poet can't tell the difference between the bad and good in generalship. The point, though, is that mimetic art in Plato's theory is necessarily an imitation of a real particular, so that strictly speaking there is no fiction in art.

Aristotle in his *Poetics* thought poets to be imitators, too, though not of mere appearance.[12] He tells us that art imitates "action," and one thing he meant by this is that the tragic poet is first and foremost a maker of plots. Now tragic plots, Aristotle believed, nearly always derive from actual incidents. (The singular exception to the general rule that tragic poets draw on history is the *Antheus* of Agathon. "Both the names and the events of that play are fictitious, yet it is enjoyable nonetheless.") Aristotle thus accepts at face value that the legends on which the tragedies are based are historical truths. But he also thinks there is an aesthetic reason to stick to the "historical" legends. "The reason is that what is possible is convincing, and we are apt to distrust what has not yet happened as not possible, whereas what has happened is obviously possible, else it could not have happened." The poet does not tell "all that happened" to someone; but rather constructs a sequence of events that makes "one action . . . the various incidents must be so constructed that, if any part is displaced or deleted, the whole plot is disturbed and dislocated"; he can "neither begin nor end haphazardly" but must connect events "in accordance with what is probable or inevitable." This raises the poet above the historian (who tells all that happened, does not discover the probable causes of events) and makes poetry "more akin to philosophy." By discovering the underlying unity of events, the poet presents, through drama, "general truths." What arouses pity and fear in the audience for tragedy is in large part the inevitability of the events of the tragic hero's passage from happiness to misery. But Aristotle's emphasis is that such *inevitability* is aided and abetted by the connection of the plot to things that actually happened.

But this has consequences for fictionality. As long as, say, the people and events of *Oedipus the King* are taken to be real by their audience, and Aristotle thinks both that these are real and that the audience takes them to be real, there is no paradox in responding with horror to Oedipus's realization that it is he who killed Laius and that Jocasta is his own mother. In Aristotle's account, the audience who takes Oedipus and his appalling situation to be real is not making a mistake. Far from it. They are enjoying the plausibility Sophocles built into the play by basing it on "what actually happened." Such an audience will not raise the specter of paradox, for they will view, according to Aristotle, *Oedipus the King* as a

---

12. The translation of Aristotle's *Poetics* used is by G. M. A. Grube, in *Aristotle On Poetry and Style* (New York: The Library of Liberal Arts, 1958), 18–19.

modern audience views *Schindler's List*, namely as theatrical docudramas of real incidents, condensed perhaps, though in the main accurate and not fictional.

The nearly exclusive concern of eighteenth-century aesthetics is the operations of what we can broadly call "taste," namely, an internal sensibility that responds to the perception of objects. Francis Hutcheson's remarks are typical.

> Those ideas which are raised in the mind upon the presence of external objects, and their acting upon our bodies, are called sensations. . . . Many of our sensitive perceptions are pleasant, and many are painful. . . . Let it be observed that . . . the word beauty is taken for the idea raised in us and a sense of beauty for our power of receiving this idea. . . . [T]he ideas of beauty and harmony . . . are necessarily pleasant to us. . . . The figures which excite in us the ideas of beauty seem to be those in which there is uniformity amidst variety.[13]

Apart from the pains and pleasures excited by external objects, no other feelings come into play in Hutcheson's theory. Even when narrative is mentioned, it is not to meditate on its fictionality but on the pleasures it gives rise to. Here is a typical passage in this vein from Edmund Burke:

> It is true, that one man is charmed with *Don Belianis* [an anonymous "pulp fiction" of 1673], and reads Virgil coldly; whilst another is transported with the *Aeneid*, and leaves *Don Belianis* to children. These two men seem to have a taste very different from each other; but in fact they differ very little. In both these pieces, which inspire such opposite sentiments, a tale exciting admiration is told; both are full of action, both are passionate; in both are voyages, battles, triumphs, and continual changes of fortune. The admirer of *Don Belianis* perhaps does not understand the refined language of the *Aeneid*.[14]

---

13. From Francis Hutcheson's *An Inquiry into the Original of Our Ideas of Beauty and Virtue* (1725), as excerpted and printed in George Dickie and Richard Sclafani, eds., *Aesthetics: A Critical Anthology* (New York: St. Martin's Press, 1977).

14. Edmund Burke, *A Philosophical Inquiry into the Origin of Our Ideas of the Sublime and Beautiful*, as excerpted in Hazard Adams, ed., *Critical Theory Since Plato* (New York: Harcourt Brace Jovanovich, 1971), 307. Burke goes on to claim that while the "principles" of taste are the same in all people (that is, the causal laws by which objects cause sentiments of pleasures or displeasures are universal), there is here and there a "weakness" of taste as when our feelings are "blunt," our passions too "violent and tempestuous," our minds too occupied in "the low drudgery of avarice," and various other deficiencies.

It is noteworthy that Burke omits any mention of the ordinary emotions—fear, admiration, repugnance, compassion, awe—that narratives such as the *Aeneid* or *Don Belianis* might arouse. The only sentiment at issue is admiration (or liking) for the work itself, not emotions toward its (real or fictional) characters.

There is one exception to the general trend of eighteenth-century aesthetics, and it is telling that it comes from someone who is more literary critic than philosopher of beauty. Samuel Johnson may well have been the first ever to raise the paradox, which he does in his 1765 *Preface* to his edition of the plays of Shakespeare.[15] Against those who condemn Shakespeare for disobeying the "unities" of time and space (according to which the action of a proper play must take place within the span of a day, and all in the same place), Johnson writes, "The objection . . . supposes that when the play opens the spectator really imagines himself at Alexandria and believes that his walk to the theater has been a voyage to Egypt, and that he lives in the days of Antony and Cleopatra." On the contrary, "the spectators are always in their senses, and know, from the first act to the last, that the stage is only a stage, and that the players are only players."

But Johnson begins to sense what he calls a "fallacy" looming, when he inquires into the origin of our reactions to the suffering or evils done during the play. Why, if the stage is only a stage and the players only players, should we be moved by the plights of what we believe to be fictions? "The reflection that strikes the heart is not, that the evils before us are real evils, but that they are evils to which we ourselves may be exposed." The fallacy would be to attribute unhappiness to the stage players, when the truth is that "we fancy ourselves unhappy for a moment." The paradox is next raised in the nineteenth century by Samuel Taylor Coleridge, whose solution is given in the famous phrase "the willing suspension of disbelief," a conception that he used specifically to argue against Johnson. I will discuss Coleridge's views at greater length in Chapter 6.

The paradox really comes into its own in the twentieth century, and this, I think, is because some of the central documents in early analytic philosophy turn on questions of existence and reference. Bertrand Russell's seminal paper "On Denoting" forced philosophy onto the issue of nonexistence: How is it we can speak meaningfully both of the author of *Waverly* and of the present king of France? Once the fact of nondenoting singular

---

15. The edition of Johnson's *Preface* consulted is the collection edited by W. K. Wimsatt, *Samuel Johnson on Shakespeare* (New York: Hill and Wang, 1960).

terms is brought out as a central item for philosophical discussion, it is only a matter of time before nonexistence and singular terms in fiction are taken up as issues in aesthetics: for example, in a 1933 Aristotelian Society Symposium by Ryle, Braithwaite, and Moore on "Imaginary Objects," and the 1954 Symposium on "The Language of Fiction," with Margaret Macdonald and Michael Scriven.[16] The time was now ripe for Colin Radford and Michael Weston's Aristotelian Symposium on the paradox.

16. G. Ryle, R. B. Braithwaite, and G. E. Moore, "Imaginary Objects," *Proceedings of the Aristotelian Society*, supp. vol. 12 (1933); Margaret Macdonald and Michael Scriven, "The Language of Fiction," *Proceedings of the Aristotelian Society*, supp. vol. 27 (1954).

is emotion toward fiction irrational?

Colin Radford thinks that the falsehood in the paradox set is propostion 2.[1] This proposition asserts that *any* person experiences an emotion only if he believes that the object of his emotion both exists and exhibits at least some of the emotion inducing properties specific to that emotion. Radford thinks that "our being moved in certain ways by works of art, though very 'natural' to us and in that way only too intelligible, involves us in inconsistency and so in incoherence."[2] Radford says that a belief that something can harm us "is a necessary condition of our being unpuzzlingly, rationally, or coherently frightened."[3] But suppose we are frightened by a threatening character we believe to be fictional; and because we believe him to be fictional, we also believe he cannot harm us. On

---

1. Colin Radford and Michael Weston, "How Can We Be Moved by the Fate of Anna Karenina?," *Proceedings of the Aristotelian Society*, supp. vol. 39 (1975): 67–93.

2. Radford, "How Can We Be Moved?," 78.

3. Colin Radford, "Tears and Fiction," *Philosophy* 52 (1977): 210.

Radford's view, we are thereby puzzlingly (inconsistently, irrationally, or incoherently) frightened. The proposition Radford endorses can be put this way:

2a. It is only the *fully rational, consistent, and coherent* person who feels emotions when he believes that the object of his emotion both exists and exhibits at least some of the emotion inducing properties specific to that emotion.

Proposition 2a is consistent with propositions 1 and 3, and if 2a is correct, the paradox is dissolved.

No one other than Radford himself has defended this conclusion in print. Radford's is still a school of thought with one student. Still, despite all the ink and paper over Radford's theory (five articles critical of Radford and five responses from him in the journal *Philosophy* alone), the issue has not been, to my mind, completely resolved. Part of the problem lies with Radford's critics who too often think his conclusion wrong just because it runs against their own intuitions. However, his critics often merely *assert* the implausibility of this claim, as when, for example, Barrie Paskins claims to find no "oddity" in having "a nice cry over the fate of Anna Karenina."[4] In one response to criticism, he calls "the inability to be critical of the coherence and rationality of a belief or way of behaving which is institutionalized in a culture" a "fault in a philosopher."[5] In another, he says it is "the worst sort of *trahison de clerc* for a philosopher to think that if most of us are unpuzzled by something and do not doubt its coherence or rationality, no one can properly do so."[6]

On this Radford is correct. It is quite properly part of the philosophical stance to consider anything, including entrenched "unpuzzling" beliefs and practices, as controversial. One of the difficulties in teaching philosophy is precisely to impart this stance, to get students to see that something that is as accepted as "Art must be beautiful" or "People have souls" might well be false; or that strongly institutionalized practices such as denying marriage to people of the same gender or butchering pigs and lambs for dinner might well be morally wrong. That having been said, it only *begins* philosophy to hold something up for question. Holding some-

---

4. Barrie Paskins, "On Being Moved by Anna Karenina and *Anna Karenina*," *Philosophy* 52 (1977): 345.
5. Radford, "Tears and Fiction," 208.
6. Colin Radford, "Stuffed Tigers: A Reply to H. O. Mounce," *Philosophy* 57 (1982): 531.

thing up to question demands that arguments be made for or against what is in question. Sometimes Radford writes as if having held the practice (if we can call it that) of emoting toward fictions *up to* question was itself sufficient to throw the practice *into* question. But to assume a philosophical stance regarding emotions toward fiction is no argument that such a practice is or is not rational. What we need is some account of irrationality, incoherence, and inconsistency to decide if emoting toward fictions is irrational, incoherent, or inconsistent.

It must also be said that part of the fault lies with Radford himself in so far as he fails to draw up a more complete account of irrationality et al. Irrationality loosely deployed invites such responses as this from H. O. Mounce who asks rhetorically, "What error of fact or logic is being committed by those of us who feel sadness on reading of the death of Anna Karenina?" and continues, "It becomes . . . only too evident that there is no such error."[7] True, certain errors of fact or logic might prompt charges of irrationality; but the irrationality Radford is hinting at is not of that kind.

Radford's Arguments

I have accused Radford's critics of advancing intuitions not arguments against him. But does Radford himself have an argument? There is a short argument Radford sometimes gives in favor of his thesis. Against H. O. Mounce (the example happens to be people frightened of stuffed tigers), Radford says, "Their fear [of stuffed tigers]—though no doubt common and natural—is *irrational. For . . . there is nothing to be frightened of.*"[8] The structure of this argument is as follows:

An emoter, Ecks, fears a stuffed tiger.
But there is nothing to be frightened of (and Ecks know this).
Therefore, Ecks's fear is irrational.

The conclusion doesn't quite follow. The premises set up an abbreviated form of the paradox. What follows from these premises is, at most, that Ecks's fear is puzzling or in need of further explanation. We sometimes

7. H. O. Mounce, "Art and Real Life," *Philosophy* 55 (1980): 186.
8. Colin Radford, "Replies to Three Critics," *Philosophy* 64 (1989): 95. The same argument is repeated against Mounce in Radford, "Stuffed Tigers," 530.

use "irrational" to describe behavior we can't explain. But an absence of an explanation doesn't really prove irrationality; it only demonstrates lack of knowledge or puzzlement. The premises could entail that Ecks is irrational if they are supplemented with a theory of what it is to be irrational. Until then, the quick argument above is a non sequitur.

Radford gives another argument for his conclusion in the form of an inference to the best explanation of how it is we have emotions toward fiction. The bulk of Radford's essay is a catalogue of possible solutions to the paradox, considered and discounted. What remains—Radford's thesis—is pronounced the best explanation; but even if all has gone well to this point, a best explanation is still only the best explanation *among those considered.* (And a theory that many find compelling, Kendall Walton's theory of make-believe, comes after Radford's original article.[9]) The more alternatives that have not been considered (and discounted), the weaker the inference. This is why Radford's critics offer a view of their own in rejecting his—to show that we are not *inescapably* led to Radford's solution. Moreover, an explanation, even if the best of a certain lot, must stand up to independent critical scrutiny. We should inquire, then, whether Radford's thesis is a correct solution on its own merits (that is, apart from whether it is the only one left standing after some number of others are knocked out).

One further preliminary. Though Radford's critics (and sometimes Radford himself) treat the charges of irrationality, inconsistency, and incoherence as if they were but one thought spelled differently, I propose a somewhat different conceptual topography. I shall distinguish five different ways of being irrational, two of which are specifically inconsistency and incoherence.

Irrationality

The term "irrational" connotes a dysfunction of reason. But reason can be dysfunctional in a variety of ways. One category of the irrational is the illogical. A person is illogical when he draws wild non sequiturs from premises, refuses to draw the conclusion clearly indicated by facts at his disposal, takes bad inferences to be good ones, or the like. I don't think

---

9. Kendall Walton, *Mimesis as Make-Believe* (Cambridge: Harvard University Press, 1990).

Radford has illogicality in mind when he charges emoters with irrationality; in any event, emoters don't appear to be illogical, for allowing oneself to feel emotion from fiction is not an inferential matter. One does, often, draw inferences from the information presented in a narrative: a viewer of *North By Northwest* infers that Roger Thornhill is in some peril as he stands on the side of Highway 41 even before the plane begins to shoot at him. Still, the viewer does not infer his anxiety but rather experiences it on the basis of what he infers.

Radford, I think, intends another category of the irrational, namely, irrational behavior. Broadly speaking, behavior is irrational when there is pathology in an agent's means or his ends. There are at least three categories of such pathology:

(a) *X* is being actively pursued as the end (goal) of an agent, though *X* is an end such that if *X* were achieved *X* would almost certainly thwart other ends the agent is also pursuing, and the agent is in a position to know this. Example: I begin to spend all my time playing bridge, though this interferes with my work, infuriates my spouse, etc. This is *irrationality of conflicting ends.*

(b) *X* is being actively pursued as the end of an agent, though *X* is an end all but impossible to achieve. Example: I seriously attempt to build a stepladder to the moon. This is *irrationality of improbable ends.*

(c) *X* is intended as a means toward an agent's end, but is such that *X* is quite unlikely to advance that end, the agent should have know this (was in a position to know this). Example: I snub and insult my boss in order to get a promotion. This is *irrationality of clearly inadequate means.*

Does the having of emotions toward fictions involve or imply any of these kinds of irrationality? I'll discuss (a) through (c) below. Two other varieties of irrationality involving action will be discussed in the sections following.

Certainly, given the right circumstances, emotions toward fictions may exhibit some means-ends irrationality.

(a′) I attend a horror film because of the emotions I expect from the film—I'm addicted to experiences of fear—though I know I will miss a crucially important interview for a job I've been wanting very much; and to top it off, I'm unemployed at the moment. This is an *irrationality of conflicting ends.*

(b′) I make it my chief goal in life, the goal on which I harness my happiness, to read every novel ever written and to see every movie ever made, and this in order (as I put it to myself) to experience the whole gamut of emotions. Since no one's life is long enough to do this, and since I still have to work eight hours a day to earn a living, my goal is irrational: it is an *irrationality of improbable ends*.

(c′) I suffer from hair loss, and decide that this is due to being all stuffed up with emotion. So I continually engage myself with novels and films in order to emote and thereby stop my balding through catharsis. This is an *irrationality of inadequate means*.

It will be easily agreed, however, that these cases are highly eccentric; they certainly don't imply irrationality in having emotions toward fictions in general. They hardly help Radford's blanket claim that *all* emoters toward fiction are irrational. One way to show this is to argue that there is some end all rational people have such that emoting toward fictions somehow thwarts that end. Plato attempted to demonstrate an irrationality of conflicting ends in the *Republic,* Book X. The overture to the Book X argument consists of some familiar bits from the earlier books: happiness is a harmony among the parts of the soul (reason, emotion, and will); such harmony is achieved only if reason is allowed to dictate behavior (only if the individual acts from reason); reason cannot dictate behavior if it is overwhelmed or confused by emotion; and, of course, we all desire happiness. One of the chief claims of Book X is that because the poet aims precisely at bringing on emotion in his audience (this being the side on which his bread is buttered), "the poet ministers to the satisfaction of that very part of our nature whose instinctive hunger [is] to have its fill of tears and lamentations,"[10] thereby tipping the psychic scales in favor of emotion against reason and ultimately—here is the conflict of ends—thwarting the happiness we all desire.

Plato cannot have meant that just one poem will nix happiness for good. He cannot have meant that because that is a silly view.[11] Plato's view

---

10. In the translation by Francis M. Cornford, *The Republic of Plato* (London: Oxford University Press, 1941).

11. Plato cannot have meant it for another reason. If emotional involvement with mimetic art were on every occasion in conflict with happiness—if this were the conclusion of *Republic* X—then Book X would be inconsistent with Book III, in which Plato ponders over the kinds of music and poetry that should properly figure in the education of the eventual guardians of the republic, the implication being that there are at least some instances of mimetic art that do not hinder proper moral development.

achieves some plausibility only when we take him to be saying that *too much* exposure to poetry will enhance emotion and bring on psychic disharmony. How much is too much? Doubtless Plato thought that his fellow citizens took in too much poetry, so the average annual dose of poetry for the average fourth-century-B.C. Athenian is too much. I belabor this to show that not even Plato will help Radford who implies that any *single* case of emoting toward fiction betrays irrationality. In any event, there is no evidence whatsoever that Radford sides with Plato on the nature and cause of unhappiness. For then Radford would have to urge that all sorts of emotional arousal not having to do with fiction—rejoicing at births, crying at weddings, being angry at injustice, etc.—will lead to unhappiness, and this Radford doesn't even hint at.

Inconsistency

Behavior can also be irrational when there is a kind of contradiction between the agent's beliefs and actions.

(d) *X* is done against the agent's explicit beliefs. Example: I believe that ghosts, even if they existed, would be immaterial spirits; yet I set up cameras trying to photograph one nonetheless. This is *inconsistency*.

Are emoters inconsistent as Radford maintains? Do they, that is, act against an explicit belief?

> It may be of some sort of comfort, as well as support for my thesis, to realise that there are other sorts of situation in which we are similarly inconsistent, i.e., in which while knowing that something is or is not so, we spontaneously behave, or even may be unable to stop ourselves behaving, as if we believed the contrary. Thus, a tennis player who sees his shot going into the net will often given a little involuntary jump to lift it over. Because he knows that this can have no effect it is tempting to think that the jump is purely expressive. But almost anyone who has played tennis will know that this is not true. Or again, though men have increasingly come to think of death as a dreamless sleep, it was pointed out long ago . . . that they still fear it. . . . But how can this appall? There is, literally, nothing to fear.[12]

12. Radford, "How Can We Be Moved?," 78–79.

The tennis player would seem to act (when he jumps) contrary to his beliefs; the person afraid of death emotes (fears), also contrary to his beliefs. Now of course *if* emoters are like either of the two supposed analogies, then emoters are inconsistent.

In order for these analogies to get off the ground, we must grant that both the tennis player when he hops and the emoter when he emotes *act* in order to charge either with acting inconsistently with their beliefs. Action paradigmatically begins with deliberation, considers various alternative courses of actions, and is put into play with a decision and enactment of one alternative in preference to the others. Neither the tennis player's jump nor the emoter's feeling pity for Anna Karenina quite meet the paradigm of an action. The tennis player jumps without really thinking about it, while the emoter doesn't deliberate over which emotion he should feel. Yet the jump and the emotion are not entirely simply autonomic reflexes, like sneezing or blushing. After all, the tennis player need not have jumped, and that the emoter need not have felt pity (either could have controlled himself). And perhaps this is enough to put both into the arena of action.

The tennis player, then, acts with the intent to help the ball over the net, though he cannot believe that this will really work. Hence, he seems to both believe and disbelieve that his little hop will help the ball. The emoter pities Anna Karenina. How does this reveal inconsistency? It is tempting to think that Radford thinks that the emoter's pity betrays an implicit belief that Anna Karenina is real (and really suffering), which would be inconsistent with the emoter's explicit belief that Anna Karenina is not at all real (and not really suffering)—the emoter would, then, both believe and disbelieve that Anna Karenina is real. But Radford explicitly rejects the idea that emoters ever take fictions to be real, as this would "turn adults into children."[13]

With which belief is emotion toward fiction inconsistent? On Radford's account, it can only be the emoter's belief that the fictional character or situation—Roger Thornhill's cornfield predicament, Anna Karenina's suicide, and so on—is unreal, nonexistent, false, not really happening, and the like. We'll suppose that (1) Ecks feels anxious over Roger Thornhill's fate as Thornhill is buzzed by a flying crop duster; and (2) Ecks believes that Roger Thornhill is a fictional character and his predicament not real. But these do not, at least taken by themselves, describe a case of someone

---

13. Ibid., 71.

doing something that is inconsistent with his beliefs. Of course, if we add the claim (3) that a person can't feel anxious over Roger Thornhill's fate unless he believe him to be in danger, then we have a contradiction among (1), (2), and (3). But this needn't point to an inconsistency among Eck's beliefs, for Ecks need not believe (3) at all.

Were Ecks also to believe that feeling anxious over Roger Thornhill's fate—or the fate of any fictional character—to be imprudent (pointless, unhealthy, a waste of time, or the like), then Ecks would be acting inconsistently with one of these beliefs. This would put Ecks on a par with the tennis jumper who jumps to help the ball over the net and believes that this cannot be done. But Ecks needn't believe that feeling anxious for a fictional character's fate is imprudent, and indeed few if any emoters hold such a belief.

It doesn't, by the way, matter if it is *true* that emoting toward fictions is imprudent, at least for purposes of consistent action. It matters only what one *believes* to be imprudent. There may be actions that are so imprudent that the rational person, by definition as it were, believes that they are imprudent. Someone who, say, jumped naked into icy ocean water might with justification be accused of irrational action, whether or not he believed that doing so was bad for his health. Either he believed this and irrationally did it anyway, or irrationally failed to believe it. However, it is not self-evidently irrational to allow oneself to have emotions toward fictions is. Emoting toward fiction *seems* at worst harmless, possibly even beneficial, even if on deep reflection or on the accumulation of empirical evidence, emoting toward fictions turns out to be, to our surprise, somehow bad for one.

There is another disanalogy between the tennis player's jump and the emoter's emoting toward fiction. We assume that people are on the whole rational, that they act on the whole consistently with their beliefs. We may think the tennis player's jump irrational, though we don't think it discredits the tennis player's *general* rationality. We allow little blips of irrationality to pop up now and then in someone's behavior without imputing some wholesale irrationality. Perhaps we would regard the player's jump as a bit endearing, something that shows him to be imperfect, hence human. If there were much more to it—if the tennis player spent hours before every game making offerings before a little shrine to a tennis god that he claims he doesn't believe in—we would tend to doubt his general rationality. Now spectators of fiction engage in emotional participation with fictional characters for hours at a time, over and over again. Were Radford to get an analogy going to capture the emoter's prolonged repetitions, he would have to summon up the tennis player fussing for hours in front of his little shrine. But the tennis player now looks *far* too irrational to count as an analogue to the emoter toward fiction—which suggests that the emoter toward fiction isn't really irrational after all.

Suppose I think—or even say out loud—"Don't go in that barn!" to the fictional teenagers about to enter the barn where the crazed psycho waits with the chainsaw. There is a playful and a serious sense in which I can think or say this: in the playful sense, I do not make a serious attempt to communicate, much like talking to oneself is not a serious attempt to communicate; in the serious sense, I will actually try to reach the fictional teenagers, and this, being impossible, imputes a little bit of irrational behavior, much like the tennis player's little jump. It is, of course, possible to exhibit more than a little bit of irrationality. I can rationally pity Anna Karenina, but I cannot rationally try to avert her suicide, since if I take her to be a fictional character, I know that there is no one who is about to jump under a train. Now this goes beyond *emoting* toward fictions; it is an example of attempting to interact with fictions; and while irrational, attempts to interact with what one takes to be fictions is not on par with having emotions toward fictions.

Incoherence

Another sort of irrationality we can attribute to someone's action is incoherence.

(e) *X* is done consciously and voluntarily, but *X* seems to serve no purpose, seems not to fit into the agent's mean-end schema at all. Example: I climb up to the roof and stay there all night. When asked why I can say only that I don't know. This is *incoherence*.

As I've defined it, incoherence is a kind of irrationality in so far as we can't figure out what end an agent could be aiming at. A man wears two neckties; "incoherent" we think for we can't for the life of us explain it. However, it is hard to tell where the incoherence resides, in us or in the man. Is he truly aiming at no end at all? Or is it just we who are baffled? Freud has provided us with a treasury of incoherent acts (and his own explanations or unmaskings of them) in the *Psychopathology of Everyday Life*. Here is one example:

> A woman traveled to Rome with her brother-in-law, a renowned artist. The visitor was highly honored by the German residents of Rome, and among other things received a gold medal of antique origin. . . . After she had returned home she discovered in unpacking that—without knowing how—she had brought the medal home with her. She immediately notified her brother-in-law of this by letter, and informed him that she would send it back to Rome the next day. The next day, however, the medal was so aptly mislaid that it could not be found and could not be sent back.[14]

This whole business seems incoherent—Why did the woman pack the medal? Why did it get mislaid again?—incoherent, that is, until Freud offers the explanation that the woman perceived that "her brother-in-law did not sufficiently appreciate the value of this beautiful gift" and thereby unconsciously "wished to keep the medal herself."

Emotion toward fictional characters is not on its face incoherent—not like wearing two ties or packing your brother's prize medal "without knowing how." Still, in a philosophical inquiry, we should be wary about accepting things at face value. We should ask what ends if any such emotion serve; and if there are no ends, we should be prepared to acknowledge that upon deeper reflection, emotion toward fiction is incoherent after all. Aristotle claimed that being brought to feel pity and fear for the tragic hero promoted a catharsis of these emotions which (perhaps adding a bit to what Aristotle said) is a process that is good for us, since it purges us of feelings potentially destructive to our happiness. At the other pole there is the view (in his essay "Of Tragedy," Hume attributes such a view to the Abbé Dubos) that what most people aim at by involving themselves emotionally with fiction is a bit of harmless pleasure from mental stimulation, much like what one gets from a game of cards.[15] More recently, Susan Feagin makes a case that artworks develop our capacities

14. Sigmund Freud, *Psychopathology of Everyday Life*, trans. A. A. Brill (New York: Mentor Books, 1951), 125.

15. Hume wrote, "L'Abbé Dubos, in his reflections on poetry and painting, asserts, that nothing is in general so disagreeable to the mind as the languid, listless state of indolence into which it falls upon the removals of all passion and occupation. To get rid of this painful situation, it seeks every amusement and pursuit" ("Of Tragedy," from *David Hume: Selected Essays*, ed. Stephen Copley and Andrew Edgar [New York: Oxford University Press, 1993], 126). The work referred to is *Réflexions critiques sur la poésie et la peinture* (1719–33) by Jean-Baptiste Dubos.

for emotion and feeling—give us what she calls "affective flexibility"—in order "to alter our sensitivities, not simply respond by using the ones we already have."[16] This idea is an appealing way of illuminating the commonplace that fiction enlarges our lives.

Whether we are purged, pleasured, or made flexible from emotions matters little for my point. Some emoters may aim at catharsis in seeking out fiction, some at affective flexibility, others at pleasurable stimulation. Any of these counts as an end that renders emotion coherent. Some— probably most—emoters have no specific end in mind when they involve themselves in fiction. They read the novel or watch the film for whatever comes. Such people take what comes, much like a traveler who isn't quite sure what's coming next, though he has no reason to believe he is in danger and looks forward to whatever is around the corner. Some emoters believe only that the experience of fiction will not harm them and may give them some pleasure or maybe some knowledge or insight. It is not incoherent to take an action whose ultimate effects are not known in advance so long as one has reason to believe these effects are likely to be benign. (It is not incoherent to open a present knowing only that one will get something which may be delightful and which will at worst be distasteful.)

I can find, then, no conception of irrationality, incoherence, or inconsistency under which a person having emotion toward what he takes to be fiction is irrational, or incoherent, or inconsistent. This, I hasten to point out, means only that Radford is wrong in his solution to the paradox. It doesn't in itself provide a solution.

16. Susan Feagin, "Valuing the Artworld," in Robert J. Yanal, ed., *Institutions of Art: Reconsiderations of George Dickie's Philosophy* (University Park: Penn State Press, 1994), 64.

three

emotion toward
fiction or fact?

Is it Anna Karenina we pity? The group of views I
call Factualism contends that the answer is—in
fact, must be—no. According to proponents of these
views, emoters do not have emotions toward *fictions*;
our emotions, ostensibly taking as their object something nonexistent, in fact take something actual as
their object. Some Factualists begin not by rejecting
Radford's claims that emotions toward fictions are irrational but, in reality, by accepting them as the beginning of an argument: Were we to feel pity for a fictional
character, we would indeed be irrational; but we're
really not irrational when we exhibit emotions generated by hearing tales of Anna Karenina and the like; so
our emotions don't really take fictions as their objects.
It isn't Anna Karenina we pity but rather _____,
where the name of some actual thing fills in the blank.
If correct, we have a solution to the paradox, for emotions toward actual things aren't *paradoxical*. In terms
of the paradox set, the Factualists propose to solve the
paradox by denying its first proposition, which is:

1. Some people (we'll call them emoters) on occasion experience emotions toward characters or situations they take to be fictions.

The real truth according to the Factualist is rather this:

1a. Emoters experience emotions *apparently* toward what they take to be fictions. But emoters *really* experience emotions toward certain actualities suggested by those fictions.

The Factualist must argue the two parts of his solution: what these actualities are (and how they are suggested by fiction); and how it is that the emoter is (nearly) always under the illusion that it is the fictional character, Anna Karenina or whoever, that is the object of his emotion.

As with any putative solution to the paradox, Factualism must present itself as a *general* solution. That is, it must insist on proposition 1a as a universal truth. A view that maintains that here or there, now and then, we have emotions putatively toward fictions though really toward actualities, is not without interest, though cannot be a general solution to the paradox. Jerrold Levinson, for example, holds that

> a novel, movie, or play may end up evoking my sadness at the death of children, my pity for starving people, my anger at racial prejudice, my contempt for politicians, etc. And these things—children's deaths, starving people, racial prejudice, politicians—do actually exist. Otherwise put, our emotions toward social phenomena or situation types or categories of persons may quite intelligibly be engaged by the course and particulars of fiction.[1]

This isn't truly a Factualism, for Levinson does not claim (nor does he intend to claim) that a novel, movie, or play *always* ends up evoking emotions for things that actually exist.

Factualism proper comes in two broad varieties: (a) views that claim that our emotions, ostensibly toward fictions, are actually toward analogues of those fictions—"people like Anna Karenina," in Barrie Paskins's phrase; and (b) views that hold that we emote not over the fictional situations presented by the narrative but over certain truths about the world some-

---

1. Jerrold Levinson, "Making Believe," in Jerrold Levinson, *The Pleasures of Aesthetics: Philosophical Essays* (Ithaca: Cornell University Press, 1996), 305. This remark occurs in what Levinson calls a "Postscript" to the essay, which is on the whole an endorsement of Kendall Walton's theory of make-believe.

how implied or embedded in the narrative—"conceptions of life" in
Michael Weston's theory. Near the end of this chapter I'll discuss Counterfactualism, not strictly a Factualism at all, but a view that bears a family
resemblance to Factualism.

People Like Anna Karenina

"In defense of the (coherence of) the tears we shed for Anna," Barrie
Paskins in a brief reply to Radford advocates a kind of Factualism. (I pass
over his attempt at a distinction between the essentially and the inessen-
tially fictional: it is muddled, and his main claim can be made without it.)
Our pity for (say) Anna Karenina "can without forcing be construed as,
pity for those people if any who are in the same bind."[2] The same for the
fictional character Cleopatra, of Shakespeare's *Anthony and Cleopatra*:
"We first feel pity, wonder, admiration, horror, affection, etc., for those if
any who are like Cleopatra and in her situation and then, on the assumption that there are none such, regret the lack [he means: "We feel the
world to be poorer for the nonexistence of Cleopatras"].["][3]
  One of the first questions raised against this view is: Who and where are
these Anna Karenina-like people, these actual doppelgängers of Cleopatra,
Roger Thornhill, Dracula, and the rest? Radford tries a *reductio ad absur-
dum* of Paskins's view on just this question: "When you are moved to tears
by Anna, you are not moved by her, at least, not *really*; but by the similarly
awful fate of Mrs. Muriel Parsons, of Belsize Park (of whom of course you
may not have heard) who in 1937, etc."[4]
  Perhaps Paskins is not saying that in apparently pitying Anna Karenina
we really pity a certain actual individual *who is known to us*. We pity
something a bit different, namely, *people like Anna* or *people in similar
straits*. It is possible to pity "the homeless" without benefit of acquain-
tance with any homeless individual. And, of course, in pitying "the homeless," we pity (I take it) each and every homeless individual. This is a kind
of response to Radford, but Paskins is not out of the woods yet. For if we
don't know of any particular person (not "Mrs. Muriel Parsons of Belsize

2. Barrie Paskins, "On Being Moved by Anna Karenina and *Anna Karenina*," *Philosophy* 52
(1977): 346.
  3. Paskins, "On Being Moved," 347.
  4. Colin Radford, "The Essential Anna," *Philosophy* 54 (1979): 391.

Park," and not Aunt Patience, and not the woman next door, and not . . . etc.) who is in Anna Karenina's bind, why should we think *anyone* is in Anna Karenina's bind, hence that there is anyone out there to be pitied (for being in her straits)?

Here's a theory: Maybe the general plausibility of a work of art—*Anna Karenina*, say—can inspire a kind of belief in its readers that there are (were) such women in such general circumstances and can inspire this belief without readers being in fact acquainted with *individuals* in Anna Karenina–like circumstances. A work that is plausible is a work that is true to life or true to how the world operates. A plausible work of fiction might be said to give rise to beliefs about the circumstances actual humans are in. On this theory, it is the very plausibility of Tolstoy's novel (and nothing else) that inspires its reader to believe that there must be people like Anna Karenina. These readers are thereby enabled to pity "such women," without these readers being able to pinpoint actual individuals who are the objects of their pity.

I think we sometimes believe that there must be people like those described in a novel, and believe this on the sheer force of the novel's plausibility. Knowing next to nothing about life among the aristocracy in nineteenth-century Russia outside of what I read in Tolstoy's fictional works, I am nonetheless convinced that there were women like Anna Karenina: at least I believe that women who left the confines of conventional marriage were certainly in grave social danger. In addition, there are works that are (that we take to be) virtual historical accounts, such as Solzhenitsyn's account of life in Stalin's prison camps, *One Day in the Life of Ivan Denisovich*, a work of fiction for which there is independent evidence of its general veracity. There is, that is, independent evidence that there were people in Ivan Denisovich's position.

If we are led, either through a work's internal plausibility or through independent evidence, to suppose there are people substantially like characters in that work, we end up pitying not an individual but a type: people like Anna Karenina, or people unlucky in love, or people entrapped by social convention, or however we specify the type of person that is "like" Anna Karenina. But we do not feel as strongly for a type as we do for individuals. I may pity the homeless in general, but as a matter of fact, once I become acquainted with a homeless person I pity *him* more strongly than I pity "the homeless." And this seems to be one problem with Paskins's view. The pity I feel for Anna Karenina seems stronger, more vibrant, and focused than the pity I might feel for those anonymous women in loveless marriages who have fallen in love with a dashing army officer and still remain miserable.

There is another problem. Not every fictional character has real counterparts that are like that character. Dracula is one. Nearly no reader of a vampire tale or viewer of a vampire movie thinks there are vampires in reality, i.e., powerful individuals who are undead and who wander the earth drinking the blood of the living. Such people still fear Dracula. Can Paskins explain this? He could, I suppose, bite the bullet and argue that while there are no vampires as such, there are manipulative, exotic, *louche* people like Dracula, and it is *these* people who are feared by readers of Bram Stoker's novel. But this is beginning to stretch credibility. Yet even if this much is granted, what shall we say of those who feel anxiety for Roger Thornhill pursued by the crop duster in *North By Northwest*? That the audience feels anxiety for those in a similar bind? Brief consideration will tell us: There is no one in a similar bind—unless we want to say we feel anxiety for anyone in danger from crop dusters or anyone in danger, period. But the first verges on the comic, while the second unacceptably dilutes Paskins's view.

Truths About Our Lives

Michael Weston says that emoters respond to the "conceptions of life" expressed by the work of fiction; Peter McCormick thinks works of fiction make "metaphorical reference" to facts about our own lives.[5] I take these to be, essentially, the same view, differing only in how these conceptions or facts are arrived at. The ancestor of the Weston-McCormick view is Samuel Johnson, who wrote of emotion toward the unhappy characters of Shakespeare's plays, "The reflection that strikes the heart is not, that the evils before us are real evils, but that they are evils to which we ourselves may be exposed."[6]

Weston, in responding to Colin Radford, agrees that "in reading a novel or watching a play we are not even under the illusion that we are

5. See Peter McCormick, "Feelings and Fictions," *Journal of Aesthetics and Art Criticism* 43 (1985): 375–83; "Real Fictions," *Journal of Aesthetics and Art Criticism* 46 (1987): 259–70; and *Fictions, Philosophies, and the Problems of Poetics* (Ithaca: Cornell University Press, 1988).

6. Samuel Johnson, Preface to *Shakespeare* (1765), reprinted in Hazard Adams, ed., *Critical Theory Since Plato* (New York: Harcourt Brace Jovanovich, 1971), 336.

attending to reportage of real people and events."[7] He also agrees (too quickly, I think) that feelings would demonstrate some "inconsistency" or "incoherence" if they were directed at *fictional* characters. Therefore, since feelings generated by fictional characters are *not* systematically "incoherent," we must be moved by something other than the predicament of those fictions.

Of John Webster's play *The Duchess of Malfi*, Weston proposes this analysis:

> If we are moved by the death of the Duchess, what, then, are we moved by? . . . Our response to the death is part . . . of our response to the thematic structure of the play, and hence to the conception of life expressed by it. We are moved, if you like, by the thought that men can be placed in situations in which the pursuit of what they perceive to be good brings destruction on both themselves and the ones they love, and that nevertheless this can be faced with a dignity which does not betray the nature of those relationships for which they perish.[8]

We can give a fairly clear account of Weston's view to a point. The *Duchess of Malfi* has, he tells us, a "thematic structure" which is (or which includes or implies) a "conception" or "vision of life." Suppose its conception of life to include the proposition that the pursuit of good sometimes brings destruction. Then to understand the play, we must grasp its thematic structure, which means that in understanding *The Duchess of Malfi* we grasp (conceive, entertain) its conception of life. But, of course, this in itself won't generate emotion. We must also believe—it must at least strike us that—this conception of life is true (of the actual world).[9] If we thought it *false*, it would not raise sorrow in us. We must also be disposed to find this factual state of affairs depressing. Finally, of course, we feel sorry that the world is unjust in this way.

---

7. Michael Weston, "How Can We Be Moved By the Fate of Anna Karenina?," *Proceedings of the Aristotelean Society*, supp. vol. 49 (1975): 82.

8. Weston, "How Can We Be Moved?," 90.

9. Weston is of two minds on whether we have to believe these "conceptions of life" to be true of the actual world before we can feel emotions. If his considered view is Factualist (and I think it is), we must believe the conceptions of life embodied in a work of fiction to be true of the actual world. But he also says that emoters respond to "a possibility of human life perceived through a certain conception of that life" ("How Can We Be Moved?," 86). Now this is not Factualist, and it doesn't, at least on its face, solve the paradox. For it is unclear how emotion could be generated simply by thinking that the world *might* be unjust.

Weston's view rests on two claims. (A) *Any* emotion engendered by a work of fiction must be caused by the conceptions of life that work expresses. We would not have a *general* solution to the paradox in a view which held that some (not all) works of fiction that aroused emotion express conceptions of life. We especially would not have a general solution to the paradox if it is admitted that every once in a while, we respond emotionally to a fictional character rather than to any conceptions of life expressed by the work in which that character appears. This would resurrect the paradox immediately. (B) Conceptions of life must be sufficiently causally dynamic to generate emotion in and of themselves, since the fictional characters (on the Weston/McCormick view) can't be the cause of emotion.[10]

(A) Weston's examples (*The Duchess of Malfi, Romeo and Juliet*) are instances of high art, and Weston's solution to the paradox not incorrectly derives from considerations about the capacity of *art* (which is not quite the same as the nature of *fiction*). Works of high art often involve meditations on the nature of love, goodness, freedom, desire, and so on. Low art, on the other hand, has no pretensions to philosophy (which is why attempts to push it into philosophy seem comic; "Crime and Redemption in the Three Stooges" is a paper that *shouldn't* be written).

"Ersatz art of a very high grade" is how Pauline Kael describes *All About Eve* in her *5001 Nights at the Movies*. Bette Davis plays an aging star (Margo Channing) who hires an adoring fan Eve Harrington (Anne Baxter) and soon discovers that the young woman is taking over her life. There *may* be a factuality symbolized here: everyone for herself in the Broadway theater. But surely our emotional responses are to Bette Davis's flashes of temperament, Anne Baxter's hypocrisy, the acerbic wit of George Sanders (as the aptly-named theater critic, Addison De Witt), and the charming naiveté of Marilyn Monroe (the starlet Miss Casswell who at a party is reluctant to call for the butler since, as she explains, someone might be named "Butler" and think she's calling for him. "She has a point. It's idiotic, but it's a point," remarks De Witt). It seems an ineluctable fact that we hope that Margo Channing triumphs and wish for Eve Harrington's downfall, emotions neither reducible to nor explainable by some response to any "conception of life."

(B) Can conceptions of life, all by themselves, bring on emotion? I have noticed that holes are a theme of Hitchcock's *Psycho*. The film opens as

10. Mike McFerren made me aware of this second aspect of Weston's view.

the camera enters the window of the Phoenix hotel room where Marion (Janet Leigh) and Sam Loomis (John Gavin) are having an adulterous affair; the dead, staring eyes of Norman Bates's (Anthony Perkins's) stuffed animals; the windows of the house overlooking the Bates Motel; the hole Norman Bates peeps through as Marion undresses; the holes made in her body as Bates in the persona of his mother stabs her in the shower; the close up of the drain as her blood runs down it followed by the shot of her eye as she lies on the bathtub floor dead; the stab wounds in insurance detective Arbogast's (Martin Balsam's) face as he pitches backward down the stairs of that house; the eye holes in the skull in the fruit cellar. I can perhaps work this up into a conception of life: *Psycho* is about holes, the absence of anything. It is about people who have no meaningful relations (the film opens with a joyless lunch-hour quickie between Janet Leigh and John Gavin). Its central protagonist is someone who isn't even himself. Its plot structure is full of comic devices turned frightful: a peep at the girl undressing, a fall down the stairs, a nagging mother. I'll summarize this by saying: *Psycho* expresses the idea that life is a meaningless comedy. Maybe this conception of life elicits from me a shudder of *angst*.

It is one thing to shudder over an abstract thought. It is quite another to shudder when "Mrs. Bates" comes into that bathroom or when Marion's sister, Lila (Vera Miles) goes into the fruit cellar. These remain emotions for a *fictional character*, and we are back in paradox. What Weston needs but does not have is an argument that I cannot shudder for Marion unless or until I am imbued with the conception of life expressed by *Psycho*. It is unlikely that such an argument will be forthcoming, for it seems rather obvious that I could shudder for both or neither or for one without the other.

Weston might respond that we don't emote over a conception of life bare; we emote over it as illustrated by the characters of the fiction that expresses it. Yet this brings back the paradox, for even if we are feeling sorry for the Duchess-as-an-instance-of-good-being-destroyed, the fact remains that this complex object is still fictional. There is no Duchess, hence no Duchess-as-an-instance-of anything. If it is paradoxical to pity the Duchess, it is no less paradoxical to pity the Duchess-as-exemplifying-a-conception-of-life.

In several papers and a book, Peter McCormick elaborates a Factualism that is substantially similar to Weston's (though considerably more prolix). Consider our feelings for the characters of Milan Kundera's *The*

Unbearable Lightness of Being, among whom are Tereza, in love with Tomas, who is incapable of commitment and who continues an "erotic friendship" with Sabina, something that tortures Tereza terribly. "Part of what moves us in Kundera's novel," McCormick writes, "is what Tereza's sufferings refer to. And this may well be the real sufferings of our families, our friends, and ourselves."[11] How does a work of fiction by a Czech author manage to "refer" to our own real sufferings? Works of fiction make "metaphorical (not literal) reference to an extralinguistic . . . domain beyond the linguistic and nondescriptive domain beyond the linguistically closed and inscribed world of the text."[12] In his book McCormick asks,

> How can such a fiction [*The Unbearable Lightness of Being*] be called gen-
> uinely instructive? Because some communities of readers come to believe,
> rightly, that a loving like Tomas's may lead to actual and intolerable suffer-
> ing. How can such a fiction be called genuinely moving? Because some
> communities of readers come to feel a genuine grief that a leaving like
> Tereza's is virtually their own. In responding imaginately [*sic*] to fiction we
> judge Tomas and ourselves, we feel for Tereza and ourselves.[13]

Fiction is "genuinely moving" because we are moved not by the suffer-ings (or whatever) of fictional entities but because we are moved by our own sufferings which the work of fiction has metaphorically denoted.

McCormick here and there suggests a kind of argument—an inference to the best explanation—for the existence of metaphorical reference. We sometimes feel instructed about actual human affairs by works of fiction. But this must mean that these works of fiction are about those human affairs. Since a work like *The Unbearable Lightness of Being* isn't literally about ourselves or our friends (Kundera knows not a single one of my circle), and since works of fiction are not one and all *romans à clef* about us in the way that Aristophanes's *The Frogs* is about Socrates or Gilbert and Sullivan's Reginald Bunthorne is in actuality Oscar Wilde, works of fiction must be nonliterally—hence metaphorically—about ourselves and our friends.

Yet imagine two ancient Athenian spectators at a performance of Sophocles's *Oedipus the King*, Literaliteis and Metaphoricos. Literaliteis finds Oedipus's persistent inquiries despite all advice to the contrary into

---

11. McCormick, "Feelings and Fictions," 381.
12. McCormick, "Real Fictions," 263.
13. McCormick, *Fictions, Philosophies, and the Problems of Poetics*, 145.

his origins to be quite anxiety producing. So does Metaphoricos, but Metaphoricos sees Oedipus's behavior as similar to human hubris, a flaw he recognizes in himself and his fellow citizens. Metaphoricos takes Sophocles's tragedy to be (metaphorically) about the human condition; Literaliteis does not. Each spectator feels anxiety, though Metaphoricos feels it from reflection on real life while Literaliteis feels it directly from a consideration of Oedipus's fictional fate. Literaliteis, we must say, isn't instructed about human affairs by Sophocles's drama. Too bad for Literaliteis, but now McCormick's view simply cannot explain Literaliteis's emotion.

A person who can't or won't grasp a metaphor—who treats Romeo's "Juliet is the sun" as a bizarre astronomical assertion—misses metaphorical meaning. It may be there, but not for him. So too for metaphorical reference. The person who doesn't see that Tereza's suffering is, metaphorically, that of himself and his friends won't respond emotionally to those factualities. But he can still respond emotionally to Tereza's sufferings (as the person who can't grasp metaphor responds to *a* meaning of Romeo's utterance). Put briefly: the paradox reappears if simply one person responds to a character as a fictional entity and not as a metaphorical pointer to some further actuality.

The Factualist's Psycho-Mechanics

The stumbling block for Factualism is that it seems to the emoter that it is the Duchess of Malfi or Tereza that he feels some emotion toward—that it is these characters or their suffering that is the object of his emotion. Or, in other words, it is natural to answer the question, Whom do you pity when reading Webster's play or Kundera's novel?, with "the Duchess" or "Tereza." This is how it seems "from the inside." Yet the Factualist must hold that this is an illusion, for he must insist that the true object of emotion—the real answer to that question—is something more along the lines of "those destroyed in their pursuit of goodness" or "those in love with cruel people," or even more simply, "ourselves" or "humanity." So there is an illusion that has to be explained away.

Hume has argued that the object and cause of our emotions need not be the same. "A man . . . is vain [proud] of a beautiful house, which belongs to him, or which he has himself built and contriv'd. Here the object of the passion is himself, and the cause is the beautiful house."[14] To take another example, I notice that my roof still leaks though I paid someone to repair it, and this causes me to become angry with the repairman. The cause (or initiating condition) of my anger is the leaky roof or my noticing that my roof still leaks, though neither of these is the object of my anger (I am not angry with the roof or myself for noticing it). The object of my anger is the repairman (or his incompetence or that I will have to have the roof repaired all over again). So it is possible for the plight of the Duchess of Malfi to be the cause of my pity without thereby and necessarily being the object of that pity. I *could* be caused by seeing a play about the plight of a character named "the Duchess of Malfi" to feel sorry that goodness is often punished in the world.

But the distinction between object and cause cannot explain away the appearance that I am sorry about the plight of the Duchess. As I see it, the Factualist has two lines of defense open: mistake and reduction. Perhaps I am mistaken about how the object of my emotion appears to me. We are not unfamiliar with situations in which a person mistakenly takes something to be the object of his emotion. Suppose I'm a bit late for work, the first time in months and months. My supervisor blows up at me. He expresses so much anger that I infer that something else is going on. My lateness *can't* be the explanation (I think). So I confront my supervisor: "You say you're angry with me but I'm only five minutes late and I'm very rarely late, and even then, it's never more than a few minutes. Could it be that you're really angry with Mr. Johnson whom you have to meet later and who is always a pain in the neck?" My supervisor might disagree (this might be resistance), or he might agree. In either case, he may well be mistaken about the object of his emotion.

The difficulty Factualism runs into is that it must claim that every emoter who claims that he feels emotion for a fictional character is *on every occasion* wrong. It's as if we had to say to *every* emoter: "Look, you think you're shedding tears over Anna Karenina; but you can't be. So you must be sorry about real people like Anna (or that such things happen in the world)." Do we have reason to think that *no one* could shed tears over Anna Karenina? Weston's reason is that Anna is fictional, hence one

---

14. David Hume, *Treatise on Human Nature*, ed. L. A. Selby-Bigge (1793; Oxford: Oxford University Press, 2d ed., 1978), book II ("Of the Passions"), section 2, p. 279. Hume held the surprising view that the object of pride and humility was always the self. It seems to me, however, that the man can be proud of himself for having built such a wonderful house, or he can be proud of the wonderful house that he has built.

couldn't cry over her fate. Not only does this beg the question in favor of Factualism; it finesses the embarrassing fact that many emoters will testify that Anna Karenina is the object of their emotion, and not people like her or some abstract truth that she exemplifies.

The Factualism might then try the avenue of reduction. He may accept the testimony that it is Anna Karenina that is the object of an emoter's pity, but claim that Anna Karenina is nothing more than some set of facts: sufferings society inflicts on women who break its rules, for example. In the way that the materialism might claim that mental events are nothing but—are reducible without residue to—brain states, the Factualist might claim that emotions toward what one takes to be fictions are nothing but emotions toward a set of actualities. There is no need to dismiss emotion toward Anna Karenina as a mistake, but now the object of the emotion is itself reduced to (reconstrued as) actualities. Yet if this means that Anna Karenina is not a fiction at all but a set of actual circumstances (a claim McCormick may endorse, though not, I think, Weston), it seems to have the untoward consequence that what we call fictional entities are really actual entities (or composites of actual circumstance), and that anyone who takes Anna Karenina to be a fiction is wrong. But what does this say of the person who takes Anna Karenina to be fictional, except that he's wrong to do so in the way that someone might wrongly take the Stanford White of *Ragtime* to be fictional? His emotions still take as their object something he believes to be fictional, and the paradox is up and running all over again.

Counterfactualism

Perhaps counterfactuals can elicit emotions. Certainly, in everyday life, we feel remorse or satisfaction over things that didn't come to pass. Someone's father dies, and he thinks: "If only dad had lived another year he and I would have taken that fishing trip we always talked about. How sad that he didn't." Or my shares of a certain stock plummet, but I hang tight until they shoot up again: "Digital Stuff just went way up. Were I to have sold yesterday, I would have lost thousands. How delighted I am that I didn't." These feelings seem to be generated by and take as their object something the emoter knows didn't happen: his father living another year, or his selling yesterday. Such circumstances seem rather commonplace, and if they are analogues to emotions toward fiction, we might have within what I'll call emotions toward counterfactuals a solution to the paradox of emotion and fiction. And there is a small class of solutions which rely in some way on counterfactuals and which I'll call Counterfactualism.

In the view of Ralph Clark, a statement ostensibly about fictional entities is to be "paraphrased" as a "complex command, or instruction, to its readers for carrying out a certain psychological task—the task of thinking what the world would be like if a certain contrary to fact sequence of events were to occur."[15] For example, this sentence from Dickens's *Martin Chuzzlewit*, "She was a fat old woman, this Mrs. Gamp, with a husky voice and a moist eye," will be paraphrased as, "Think what the world would be like, contrary to the way that it actually is, if it contained a fat old woman with a husky voice and a moist eye whose name was Mrs. Gamp."[16] Clark further thinks that the very entertaining of these counterfactual suppositions "does, or is likely to, produce feelings"—just as the parent who "suddenly, thinks to himself what it would be like if his child were kidnapped" will feel fear.[17]

The parent who thinks about his child's being kidnapped will probably feel emotion. This is similar to the examples given above. The parent thinks: Were my child kidnapped, he would be in grave danger and I would feel terrified. However, all of these examples—were dad to have lived another year, were I to have sold Digital yesterday, were this child kidnapped—are not exact analogues to fictions, for they are counterfactuals about something existent (a man, some shares of Digital Stuff, a child). True, they hypothesize something that is counter to fact about the existent thing (dad's living another year, my selling yesterday, my child's being kidnapped), but there is at least an existent thing for an emotion to hang its hat. Fiction's counterfactuals concern a world containing a Mrs. Gamp toward whom we are invited to have certain feelings. Yet there is no Mrs. Gamp. It is as if I, childless, had to both imagine that I have a child and that my child is kidnapped. Any emotional edge to these musings would seem blunted by the nesting of these counters-to-fact.

We should ask also whether this is much like our experience of fiction. The parent who imagines that his child is kidnapped construes the real world exactly like it is, except that now his child is bound up in some

---

15. Ralph W. Clark, "Fictional Entities: Talking About Them and Having Feelings About Them," *Philosophical Studies* 38 (1980): 342.
   16. Ibid., 344.
   17. Ibid., 347.

anonymous person's van, being driven over dark country roads. It is important to note—this may be obvious—that the parent must project himself into this hypothetical: the parent must conceive of himself, perhaps being exactly where he (actually) is, knowing and worrying about his child's welfare. One way for a parent to imagine his child being kidnapped is to imagine that, sitting where he is, he is waiting for news from the police.

Yet this is different from our experience of fiction. In reading *Anna Karenina* I do not imagine the world as it is, only now containing (people like) Anna, her husband, her son, and so on. There is something comically Woody Allenish about this: Anna and Vronsky dressed in nineteenth-century garb, weaving in and out of modern-day city traffic, on their way to a romantic liaison. Clark could respond: You haven't changed the world enough in imagination to accommodate the fiction. You have to "think what the world would be like," not just if it contained Anna and the rest, but if it were nineteenth-century Russia, with horse-drawn carriages not automobiles.

But what are we thinking when we think this? We are "thinking" the events of *Anna Karenina*—that is, we imagining the situations of the novel. There are two ways to understand this. There is Clark's suggestion that we imagine the actual world as if it contained all the characters and apparatus of *Anna Karenina* (Anna, nineteenth-century Petersburg, trains pulled by steam engines, etc.). Then there is a less complicated suggestion that we simply imagine the characters and situations of Tolstoy's novel. (We'll have to wait a bit to see what all this might involve.) The less complicated suggestion might well do the trick (of generating emotion), so why opt for Clark's suggestion? Is there a difference between changing (in imagination) the actual world so that it is like the world of *Anna Karenina* (Clark's suggestion) and imagining the world of *Anna Karenina*?

Clark might respond that his suggestion lends some emotional power to our imagination, since we are now imagining Anna's sufferings taking place in the actual world. Thus, in thinking what the world would be like if contrary to fact it contained exactly everything in Tolstoy's novel, we imagine Anna and Vronsky living down the block, being unhappy and the rest, then we might bring some further emotional power to our imagination— at the cost, I fear, of being untrue to our experience of fiction. Whatever is going on when I feel anxiety for Roger Thornhill of *North By Northwest* it is *not* because I think *the actual world* to be such that somewhere (where?)

and sometime (now? in 1959, when the film was released?) a man is fleeing from a crop duster. Further, unless we are losing our grip on reality, we are not imagining Anna's sufferings to be actual, so why drag in the actual world at all?

William Charlton offers another version of Counterfactualism. At first, Charlton's position seems to be a minor variation on Barrie Paskins's view. Paskins thought that when we pitied Anna Karenina we pitied "those real people, if any, in the same bind." Charlton objects that this requires that we know such real people, though we very well might not yet we will still feel pity occasioned by reading *Anna Karenina*. Charlton also thinks, rightly or wrongly, that we won't feel an emotion unless we are somehow prepared to act on (or from) that emotion. And Paskins, Charlton notes, neglects the role of action altogether in his theory.

So "I feel pity for Anna Karenina" is to be analyzed, William Charlton thinks, as "If any of my friends had a husband like Karenin or a lover like Vronsky, would that I might be able to help her to do what is best."[18] Or, suppose we are glad that Odysseus is building a raft to return to Ithaca. Then we would be in "the state of mind reflected in the sentence: 'Were a friend of mine in Odysseus's position, O that I might do nothing to interfere with his resolve.'"[19] And when we are afraid for Miss Muffet, about to be visited by a spider, we have "a conditional desire that if a real person had her reasons for action, I might help that real person."[20] Charlton's main reason for advancing the bit about desiring to help these people is a view about the nature of emotion in relation to action: "To be moved emotionally is to be moved to action."[21] But now, how can we feel emotion for things that don't exist, given that action toward them must seem absurd? Charlton then posits these counterfactuals as "reflecting" our state of mind. They take up the slack in our impetus to act, so to speak. We no longer are, absurdly, wanting to help Anna Karenina or to cheer on Odysseus or whatever, but rather preparing to help "our friends" should they ever be in Anna's or Odysseus's situation. Barry Paskins has readers of *Anna Karenina* pitying real people in her bind whoever they are. Charlton's view has emoters feeling pity for some friend, suitably

---

18. William Charlton, "Feeling for the Fictitious," *British Journal of Aesthetics* 24 (1984): 212.
19. Ibid., 213.
20. Ibid., 211.
21. Ibid., 206.

decked out as Anna Karenina or Anna Christie or Anna L. Owens (of the King of Siam fame). And who would find a puzzle in feeling emotion for a friend?

One problem with Charlton's view is that he unnecessarily links action and emotion. R. T. Allen makes the correct point, "But even when an emotion normally, in real life, includes or engenders a desire, it does not always do so, especially when we know that nothing can be done and we do not resent or feel frustrated by that fact. . . . It is precisely a fictitious event that calls for nothing to be done."[22] To this, Charlton has made the not quite convincing reply that emotion in such cases moves one to inaction.[23] Even if Allen is right (and we shall return later to the vexed topic of emotion and action), his objection knocks out only the second and less important half of Charlton's analysis; and while Allen is thereby entitled to assert, "We *feel* (not wish nor anything else) [for Anna]," he is (at least given only the point about emotion not always engendering a desire to act) *not* entitled to assert also that "we feel *for Anna* (not a real person nor Anna taken wrongly to be a real person)."[24]

Colin Radford complains that Charlton adopts an "implausible thesis," because we can be moved by thoughts of what we would feel or do were one of our friends in (say) Anna Karenina's bind and yet still feel nothing for Anna (the fictional character).[25] Charlton can mount a response to this. His analysis, remember, is a reduction: there is nothing to feelings for Anna but feelings for some-one one knows in a similar bind. If our feelings for Anna Karenina *consist in* certain thoughts about what would be the case were one of our friends in her bind, then on Charlton's analysis by feeling sympathy for one's friend imagined to be in a similar bind one has *thereby had* feelings for Anna.

The implausibility Radford smells might then be put another way: Who would think the *meaning* of "I pity Anna Karenina" to be "I pity any of my friends who were in a similar bind"? What Charlton might be better said to have is not an "analysis" at all, but an argument which begins with the

---

22. R. T. Allen, "The Reality of Responses to Fiction," *British Journal of Aesthetics* 26 (1986): 65.
23. William Charlton, "Radford and Allen on Being Moved by Fiction: A Rejoinder," *British Journal of Aesthetics* 26 (1986): 392. Charlton is not altogether clear about his view on a related point: can we today feel pity for Montezuma, a person long dead, given that it is impossible to help him (today)? He seems (though I cannot be sure) to deny that properly speaking we *feel* anything for Montezuma. See "Feeling For the Fictitious," 206; and the "Rejoinder" to Radford and Allen, 392.
24. Allen, "The Reality of Responses to Fiction," 66.
25. Colin Radford, "Charlton's Feelings About the Fictitious: A Reply," *British Journal of Aesthetics* 25 (1985): 382.

claim that one simply *couldn't* feel anything for the fictional Anna (a claim, I might add, which Radford meets halfway), proceeds to infer that we must be feeling sympathy for something else, and finally concludes that we must be feeling sympathy for a friend were she in Anna's straits. But, unfortunately for his view, the final inference is a non sequitur.

make-believe
and quasi-emotion

The Factualists argued that we do not have emotions to *fictions*. Kendall Walton in his well-received and highly influential book, *Mimesis as Make-Believe*, argues that we do not have *emotions* to fictions.[1] It is worthwhile quoting again the case of Charles:

> Charles is watching a horror movie about a terrible green slime. He cringes in his seat as the slime oozes slowly but relentlessly over the earth destroying everything in its path. . . . The slime, picking up speed, oozes on a new course straight toward the viewers. Charles emits a shriek and clutches desperately at his chair. Afterward, still shaken, he confesses that he was "terrified" of the slime.
>
> Was he terrified of it? I think not. Granted, Charles's condition is similar in certain obvious respects

---

1. Kendall Walton, *Mimesis as Make-Believe* (Cambridge: Harvard University Press, 1990). Page references in parentheses in the body of the text are to this work, hereafter cited as *MMB*.

to that of a person frightened of a pending real-world disaster. His muscles are tensed, he clutches his chair, his pulse quickens, his adrenaline flows. Let us call this physiological-psychological state quasi-fear. But it alone does not constitute genuine fear. (*MMB*, 196)

On Walton's view, it is false the Charles fears the slime, though true that he quasi-fears it. This is in part due to Charles's lack of belief that he is in danger, and Walton holds fast to the thesis that belief is required for (real) emotion. "We should be wary of the idea that people literally pity Willy Loman or grieve for Anna Karenina or admire Superman while being fully aware that these characters and their sufferings or exploits are purely fictitious," and this because "pity involves a belief (or judgment, or attitude) that what one pities actually suffers misfortune, and admiration a belief that the admired object is admirable, but the normal appreciator does not think it is actually the case that Willy suffers or that Superman is admirable" (203). Such appreciators will at most quasi-pity Willy Loman or quasi-admire Superman, just as Charles at best quasi-fears the slime (or equivalently, that Charles "fears" the slime, that he make-believedly fears it, and that it is but a fictional truth that Charles fears the slime).

Quasi-emotions can, on Walton's view, happily coexist with the absence of belief in the reality of their object (and presumably with the presence of disbelief in that reality). Instead of proposition 1 of the paradox set, Walton will affirm:

1b. Emoters feel quasi-emotions, not emotions, toward what they take to be fictions. And quasi-emotions are generated by make-belief, not by belief.

Proposition 1b is consistent with propositions 2 and 3; and 1b, if true, solves the paradox. Is proposition 1b true?

Noël Carroll objects to Walton's theory as follows. Charles confesses himself terrified, yet Walton says he is not. But now Charles would seem to be under the illusion that he is terrified, and what could the difference be between the illusion that one is terrified and being terrified?[2] "That is, even if I am under the illusion of being terrified, am I not still terrified?" But there is a difference between an unreflective, off-the-cuff observation and one that is informed by philosophical reflection, that is thought through. Charles's confession that he is terrified is, perhaps, unreflective.

2. Noël Carroll, *The Philosophy of Horror, or Paradoxes of the Heart* (New York: Routledge, 1990), 69.

And Walton has arguments that Charles is not really afraid, but only quasi-afraid.

Belief and Make-Belief

Walton thinks he can explain our appreciation of mimetic art in general, and our emotions toward fiction in particular, by analogy with children's games of make-believe. Just as children may play a game in which they make-believe that stumps are bears, appreciators of Shakespeare's tragedy *King Lear* may play a game in which they make-believe there is a King Lear who, in his old age, has unwisely divided his kingdom between the two daughters who publicly professed their love for him, who is then treated badly by those daughters, who enters a period of madness, and so on. Stumps are "props" in the children's game of make-believe, and Shakespeare's play is a prop in the adult's game. Shakespeare's play, though, is a considerably more complex prop than the stump. In particular, the play by dint of the "fictional truths" it contains "authorizes" certain games of make-believe (it authorizes us to make-believe that King Lear is aged but does not authorize us to make-believe that King Lear is blind). "Appreciating paintings and novels is largely a matter of playing games of make-believe with them of the sort it is their function to be props in" (*MMB*, 53).

The notion of make-belief usually, though not always, stands in contrast with belief. The children do not believe there is a bear, though they make-believe there is one. The audience to *Lear* does not believe there is an aged king mistreated by his daughters, though they make-believe there is one. However, spectators to *A Streetcar Named Desire* both make-believe and believe that there is a card table and cards during the poker night scene (because it is both fictionally and actually true that there are cards and a table). Not everything that is "part" of a game of make-believe is *merely* make-believe. The issue before us is what bearing make-belief without benefit of belief has on emotion, and in particular whether the fact that an emotion is generated by a game of make-believe is thereby something different enough from an emotion generated by belief to make it false that emoters toward fiction feel fear, pity, and the like.

An argument suggested by Walton is this: *Charles makes-believe that there is a dangerous slime threatening him, and on that account feels fear.*

Therefore, Charles feels make-believe fear. But this argument seems like a non sequitur. Compare: *Charles suspects that there is a dangerous slime threatening him, and on that account feels fear. Therefore, Charles feels suspect or suspicious fear.* Now there could be such a thing as suspect or suspicious fear: suspect fear might fear we're not sure is sincere, while suspicious fear can only be parsed as a combination of being suspicious and fearful. But suspect or suspicious fear isn't a *kind* of fear, and Walton needs make-believe fear to be different in kind from ordinary fear—different enough so that when someone experiences make-believe fear it must turn out to be false that he experiences fear.

While the term "make-believe" is privileged in Walton's theory, if nothing else by its appearance in the title of the book, there are other terms that Walton uses more or less interchangeably. A person who makes-believe that *p* is the case also imagines, entertains, considers, or turns over in his mind the proposition that *p* (*MMB*, 15). A person playing a game of make-believe is also said to embark on a daydream or to call up images (13). But neither of these terms makes a better argument. If a person imagines that *p* and on that basis comes to feel pity, it will not follow that he feels imaginary pity. If a person entertains the thought that *q* and thereby comes to feel horror, we will not be entitled to say that he feels entertaining horror. And so on.

It isn't that playing games of make-believe couldn't generate emotion. What I'm questioning is whether the mere fact that it is a game of make-believe that generates the emotion is sufficient to establish that the emotion generated is odd, abnormal, quasi, or make-believe. But Walton has other arguments that the emotions we have toward fictions are not quite real.

Emoter Participation and Imagining De Se

One important aspect of games of make-believe concerns what Walton terms "imagining *de se*," or imagining *of oneself* that this or that is true. As this concept is deployed, it does not merely cover the limited case in which I imagine myself to be Napoleon, or imagine of myself that I have won the lottery. I could, for example, imagine *you* to be Napoleon or that it is *you* who won the lottery, and I would still be imagining *de se*. "To imagine seeing a rhinoceros is to imagine *oneself* seeing a rhinoceros, not just to imagine an instance of rhinoceros seeing. One who imagines

Napoleon's seeing a rhinoceros . . . does not thereby 'imagine seeing a rhinoceros' as this phrase is ordinarily understood" (*MMB*, 31). Heather, a child playing a game in which stumps are bears, does not simply imagine that there is a bear there, or imagine of the stump that it is a bear; she imagines this *and* imagines herself seeing the bear. She is an onlooker (a spectator) in her game of make-believe. Her game generates (at least) the fictional truths that there is a bear *and* that Heather sees it. Indeed, it is Walton's view that *anyone* who uses a mimetic artwork as a prop in his game of make-believe introduces himself as a spectator (and that *most* games of make-believe involve imagining *de se*).

According to Walton's theory, then, what we might term the world of the work of fiction is enlarged by spectator participation. When Sherrill, a spectator at a performance of *Othello*, imagines that Iago lies to Othello, Sherrill becomes a pretend spectator to Iago's treachery. Sherrill does not exactly enter Shakespeare's play; rather the world of Shakespeare's play is enlarged to accommodate Sherrill. Appreciators of novels, plays, and films—"participants" as Walton sometimes calls them—are like "actors playing themselves" (*MMB*, 211). Sherrill, though, is an invisible participant. "The spectator of a performance of Ibsen's *Hedda Gabler* fictionally hears Hedda speak, but it is not fictional that she addresses him or speaks to him. It is not commonly fictional, in our games with representational works, that characters notice or respond to us, or that we exchange glances with them or hold conversations with them" (229). Charles watching the slime movie "is participating psychologically in his game of make-believe. It is not true but fictional that he fears the slime." Why? Because Charles "is an actor, of a sort, in his game, as well as an object; he is a reflexive prop generating fictional truths about himself" (242), among which are the fictional truths that he is in the path of the slime and that he is afraid. The argument now implied is this: *Because Charles is merely an actor playing himself as a person standing in the path of a horrible slime, any emotional reactions he has are themselves simply part of the fiction.* Is this argument sound?

It is true that an actor portraying fear need not himself really feel afraid. But it is not true that an actor portraying fear will *never* really feel afraid. A "method actor" might work himself into a lather of genuine fear, as Dustin Hoffman was said to do when portraying his character, graduate student Babe Levy, under torture by the evil Nazi dentist Szell (Lawrence Olivier—who reputedly advised the increasingly distraught Hoffman, "Try acting, dear boy"). Still, we might think that Hoffman's real emotion is an exception to the rule, and that if Charles is a typical actor and truly portraying himself as a character in the slime movie, then he is *unlikely* to feel real fear. Call the film Charles watches *It Came from the Swamp*. Suppose there is a scene in *Swamp* that contains a group of unaccredited actors (extras) fleeing from the slime. These actors might cringe and shriek at the slime's approach. Charles is (on Walton's theory) a sort of unphotographed extra in *Swamp*; and just as any (photographed) extra will likely not feel real fear as the slime's approach, neither will Charles.

But there is at least this difference. The extras run from the slime, but Charles does not (a point for Walton). But Charles afterward is shaken and confesses himself terrified, but no extra after the shot is shaken, nor says he was terrified (a point against Walton). Walton dismisses Charles's claim that he was terrified, but would Walton dismiss Dustin Hoffman's claim that he was terrified when the sadistic dentist intent on causing horrible pain approaches? We mark a difference between Hoffman's (perhaps excessive) method acting and most actors who merely portray fear, saying that Hoffman really felt afraid but most actors who portray fear do not really feel afraid. (I feel no temptation to say of such actors that they are even experiencing quasi-fear.) And we might also wish to mark a difference between Charles whose pulse races, who cringes, clutches, and shrieks, and who confesses himself terrified, with Mark, another spectator of the slime attack. Mark mugs being afraid—he too clutches at his seat, shrieks, and makes his eyes go wide—but Mark is going through such antics to amuse his friends. The only way I can see to mark off the difference is to say that Charles is really afraid and Mark is only miming or pretending fear.

There is another, deeper, difference between Charles (as typical spectator) and an actor playing a role. The actor is enjoined by his role and the other fictional propositions of the drama to say and do certain things with thus-and-such feeling, though there is often a range of interpretation permitted, and thus a range of feelings that might be expressed. Suppose Jack is cast as Hamlet. Hamlet encounters the Ghost on the battlements of Castle Elsinore and eventually this little exchange transpires.

GHOST: "Revenge his foul and most unnatural murder!"
HAMLET: "Murder!" (Act I, Scene 5, 25–26)

Jack, given the overall context of the play, should put some horror or anger in his voice. After all, the Ghost has just told Hamlet that his father did not die a natural death and asks revenge. Jack's natural responses are not to be brought into play if they run contrary to horror or anger. If Jack hates and fears his own father (he beat him as a child and continues to threaten his mother), then Jack should not utter the line "Murder!" with relief in his voice. If Jack does not believe in ghosts at all, he should not utter his responses to the ghost with a voice dripping with disbelief and sarcasm. Jack's emotional responses are constrained and dictated by Shakespeare's script.

Charles, on the other hand, even if thought of as portraying himself as an extra in the slime movie, *does* rely on his natural attitudes in his emotional responses. Richard Moran holds that our emotional responses to imagined events are often expressive of "real commitments" or "genuine attitudes." That is, they are not "what we are enjoined [by a work of fiction] to feel" but rather "what we are naturally inclined to feel."³ Put another way, our "acting" toward the events of fiction is typically reflective of our real selves. Even if in our games of make-believe we portray ourselves as spectators to fictional events, we react *as ourselves*. This implies that our emotional response to, say, Claudius's treachery is *real*, and not on a par with the other fictional truths of Shakespeare's play. And this seems correct. We rely on *our* (real) attitudes to respond emotionally, even to what we take to be fictions. Why then should the products of those attitudes, the emotions themselves, not be fully real?

The Analogy with Children's Games

Walton told us at the beginning of his book that we should look to children's games to explain our appreciation of art. And in that spirit Walton likens Charles to Timmy, a child who is playing a game of make-believe with his father. Timmy's father pretends to be a vicious monster stalking Timmy. When the father lunges at the boy, Timmy flees screaming. "But Timmy has a delighted grin on his face even as he runs, and he unhesitatingly comes back for more. He is not really afraid. But it is fictional that he is afraid" (*MMB*, 242). I think we must agree that Timmy is not really afraid, not merely because he is playing a game but because of his delighted grin. And, of course, *if* Charles is very much like Timmy, then Charles is not really afraid.

3. Richard Moran, "The Expression of Feeling in Imagination," *Philosophical Review* 103 (1994): 94–96.

Is Charles very much like Timmy? Charles, remember, clutches the arms of his chair; he cringes, shrieks, gasps for breath; his heart pounds violently; he has his heart in his throat throughout the movie (a difficult predicament, too, if it is pounding violently); and he later confesses himself terrified. Walton wants to state his case with a bit of drama: if even Charles (thus described) is not truly afraid, then no emoter toward fiction is. But it covers up differences to describe both Timmy and Charles as being in the same state, namely not afraid. There is a kind of play-fear that we can generate. It is the sort we undergo at the amusement park in haunted houses or from riding not-too-scary roller coasters. It is characterized by some gasps but with giggles too. Timmy exhibits this play fear. Charles, on the other hand, gasps but doesn't giggle. But then Charles is unlike Timmy.

There is a kind of cinematic or theatrical experience Timmy approximates. Audiences at certain B-grade chop-and-slash movies are clearly having a good time. In these movies the teenage couple leaves the group by the campfire to wander together into the woods at night. Everyone in the audience knows that the fiendish killer will get them; it's only a matter of when and how. And when he does, the audience shrieks and jumps in their seats—and then laughs. This is play fear, or more accurately the audience is startled then delighted. Pretend fear is clearly not real fear, and the audience's reactions at these movies is about what I imagine Timmy to feel. Outside of children's games, we can pretend to have emotional responses other than those we have. We can pretend grief at a funeral—we adopt a grave expression, speak with measured tones, and even bury our face in our hands at strategic points—though we feel nothing for the deceased, for example. But our responses to characters and situations we take to be fictions are not generally thus pretended. Pretend fear, on the contrary, does *not* capture Charles's experience, for as Walton describes him Charles is risking heart attack. And play emotion is not the term for what any spectator who experiences harsh emotion while watching fiction. Those of us who profoundly pity Lear cradling the dead Cordelia in his arms do not think it play pity (or indeed anything less or other than profound pity). We do not make ourselves seem to pity Lear for appearance's sake. And we do not pity Lear's plight, and then giggle.[4]

<hr>

4. Some people think that the emotions we have towards fiction must be somehow less than real because they are always pleasant and real life emotions are not always pleasant. See, for one, Marcia Eaton, "A Strange Kind of Sadness," *Journal of Aesthetics and Art Criticism* 41 (1982): 51–63. It is not obvious that this is so. In Chapter 9, I endorse a view of David Hume which has it that although

Causes and Kinds

Walton, to repeat, maintains that if it is true that Charles only quasi-fears the slime then it is false that he fears it. This implies that full-fledged emotion is different *in kind* from quasi-emotion, as different as fool's gold is from real gold, and Walton agrees:

> The "fear" experienced by Charles . . . and that experienced by Frances [really afraid of dogs], who flees from Fido, or Aaron [really afraid of flying], who, with his teeth gritted in determination, manages to go through with an airplane flight, are *animals of different kinds*. To assimilate them would be to emphasize superficial similarities at the expense of fundamental differences. A creditor might as well accept payment in fool's gold. (*MMB*, 202; emphasis added)

One reason Walton gives for the thesis that emotions toward fiction and emotions toward fact are different in kind is that they differ in cause:

> To be (really) afraid of a tornado . . . is to have certain phenomenological experiences (quasi-fear) as a result of knowing or believing that one is endangered by the tornado. What makes the state one of *fear* rather than anger or excitement is the belief that one is in danger, and what makes the tornado its object is the fact that it is the tornado that one takes to be dangerous.
>
> It is clear enough what to say about Charles if this is what fear is: He experiences quasi-fear as a result of realizing that fictionally the slime threatens him. This makes it fictional that his quasi-fear is caused by a belief that the slime poses a danger, and hence that he fears the slime. (244–45)

Charles experiences fear as a result of making-believe he is threatened; the person really afraid of a tornado experiences fear as a result of a belief that he is endangered. The question now is: Does a difference in cause indicate, in this case, a difference in kind?

In general, two things that are otherwise alike are not *different in kind* because their causes are themselves different in kind. 12 is the same

---

someone may describe his experience of seeing Shakespeare's *King Lear* as "enjoyable," it needn't be the case that his emotions were themselves pleasant, though the overall aesthetic experience of the play may have been more pleasant than not.

number whether it is derived from adding 7 + 5 or by multiplying 3 x 4.[5] Headache is headache whether brought on by hangover or by eyestrain. Two organisms are sheep even if one is generated from normal sexual intercourse and the other through cloning. A fire in a haystack is not a different thing depending on how it was started (lightning, spontaneous combustion, lantern falling over, etc.). Of course we can *describe* things in ontogenetic terms. A fire that is an "act of God" (in insurance terms) is a fire started by natural causes; arson is fire intentionally set. But no one thinks this marks any important difference in kind in the *fires* thereby brought about.

At the very least, a quasi-X must both have some important properties of a full-fledged X, and must lack other important properties. A quasi-X must fall short of being an X. It would be nonsense to call an apple a quasi-citrus fruit for an apple is not a citrus fruit at all. It would be false to call a lemon a quasi-citrus fruit for a lemon is a citrus fruit in every sense. A robot that looked (from the outside) just like a person, and who talked like a person, moved like a person, and so on, might be called a quasi-person because it lacked consciousness. A dog which doesn't look like a person but which possessed consciousness and engaged in purposive activity could also be called a quasi-person. It is in this sense that we think the robot and dog to be quasi-persons and not really persons.

Consider a man generated through cloning. What important properties of persons would he lack, save for the property of being generated by sexual intercourse? None. He is not like the robot (which looks like a person but lacks consciousness) or like a dog (which looks like a dog but is conscious and acts purposively). There would be no justification in calling such a man a quasi-person, where this would imply that he falls short of being a person. With all this background of multiplication and addition, sheep, fires, and robots, let's ask, Does Charles's fear fall short of full-fledged fear? And I think we must incline toward saying no, not if the only reason offered is that make-belief rather than belief cause his fear.

Action and Inaction

But difference in cause isn't the only reason Walton offers. We are reminded several times that Charles "does not have even an inclination to

5. Ed Gron suggested this example.

leave the theater or call the police" (*MMB*, 199, 201). Walton refers to this as Charles's "nonmotivating state," and argues that to consider "Charles's nonmotivating state to be one of fear of the slime, would be radically to reconceive the notion of fear. Fear emasculated by subtracting its distinctive motivational force is not fear at all" (201–2). Fear less its motivational force is quasi-fear. "What is pity or anger which is never to be acted on? What is love that cannot be expressed to its object and is logically or metaphysically incapable of consummation?" (196). The implied answer, of course, is that these would at best be quasi-pity, quasi-anger, and quasi-love. The quasi-emotions, then, are mere "constellations of sensations or other phenomenological experiences characteristic of real emotions, ones that the appreciator who 'pities Anna' or 'admires Superman,' for instance, shares with people who really pity or admire real people" (251). On Walton's view, emotions toward fiction are constellations of sensations less motivational force while the full-fledged emotions are constellations of sensations with motivational force.

Indeed, the apparent nonmotivationality of emotions toward fiction makes for Walton's strongest argument that emoters toward fiction don't truly experience emotions, though ironically it is the argument that least depends on the theory of make-believe. For it isn't clear *how* (or *that*) playing games of make-believe removes motivational force from the emotions such games engender. Charles *could* play a game of make-believe in which he *does* flee the theater or call the police, just as someone smitten by Princess Anne, the character Audrey Hepburn played in *Roman Holiday,* could play a game of make-believe in which he has flowers sent to Princess Anne (and I mean to Princess Anne, not to Audrey Hepburn). These might be odd (nonstandard, maybe even nutty) games of make-believe, though possible games.

Suppose Jack believes he is under attack by a charging lion, thereby feels fear, and thereby is motivated to flee. But even this far it is not clear that the motivating force comes from the belief or from the fear (from the emotion). Suppose Jack believes he is under attack by a charging lion, and (without feeling fear) is thereby motivated to flee. This does not seem psychologically impossible. So it is not entirely clear from the outset that motivation for action comes from the *emotions* aroused by belief. However, many emotions are unpleasant to experience, and perhaps the unpleasant feelings fear brings—the rapid heart rate, the dry mouth, the hyperventilating—is a motive for Jack to flee (he wants to stop the unpleasant feelings).

To be motivational, an emotion must provide a reason to act, or if not quite a reason, then a spur to act. My fear of closed spaces gives me a reason to avoid them. I don't mean that such a reason must override other considerations. I might want to see the view from the top of the Washington Monument, and discover I must ride in a small elevator to the summit. I then weigh one reason against the other. Or suppose I'm caught in a closed space. I might be spurred by my fear to get out. A spur causes action directly, without weighing the reasons pro and con.

To mark off a sharp break—a difference in kind—it must be the case that all emotions toward real things are motivational and *no* emotions toward fiction are motivational. Yet there seem cases of emotions toward real things that are nonmotivational. Suppose I've just been mugged, and am very angry with my assailant, though I sit and stew and do nothing, for I think there is nothing to do. Or I fall in love with a movie star, and again do nothing, for I realize the hopelessness of the situation. Or I admire Congressman Barney Frank but take no steps to express my admiration. Or I am stranded on a remote island, and hope that I will someday be rescued, though all I see for me to do is to sit tight and wait. "I felt a helpless sorrow" or "I felt an impotent rage" don't seem contradictory. Rather "helpless" and "impotent" point to the inactivity of the emotion; they do not *falsify* my claim to feel sorry or angry.

What, though, of our normal, everyday experiences of fiction? Don't these lack motivational force? Aren't these hotbeds of inactivity? A glance at spectators in the theater who shriek and clutch during the slime movie, and yet who stay glued to their seats seems evidence that they are not motivated to act. Yet what of Eric, who in Walton's example plays a game of make-believe in which stumps are ferocious bears, and who spots a stump and flees, screaming, away from it? Is his fear truly nonmotivational? Is my sorrow inactive though I shed tears over the dead Cordelia, and cancel our plans for an after-theater drink since the play has put me in a funk? Is Charles's when he gasps and grips the arm of his chair? Are we *sure* he hasn't even a teeny motive to leave the theater? (There's a difference between being unmotivated to act and not acting on a motive one has.)

I think that if we probe a bit more into the notion of a motivator we might find more commonality than difference between emotions toward real things and emotions toward fictions. A motivator, I've said, is either a reason or a spur to act. But such reasons or spurs must have an occasion. My fear of closed spaces gives me a reason to avoid them, though most of the time I'm not confronted with the option of entering closed spaces.

Suppose the world changed and now there were no closed spaces (though I knew myself to fear them). My fear would still give me a reason to avoid closed spaces though I have no opportunity to exercise that reason. After being mugged, I might return to my apartment and sit and do nothing, for I don't know the mugger and believe the police won't do anything. But if I were to encounter the mugger on the street again and recognize him my anger toward him would likely awaken its nascent motivating force and *now* given the opportunity I have reason to do something (yell, run, whatever).

Motivators need opportunity, and it may be that fiction arouses emotion with motivational force but will little or no opportunity to exercise it. I might in truth have a reason to express my admiration of Superman to that fictional character yet (by dint of his fictionality) never have opportunities to do so. Such an emotion would not be entirely denuded of motivation, hence would be on par with emotion toward real things. I may even wish I could comfort old Lear as he cradles his daughter, a wish that I acknowledge can't be satisfied in reality, but that presses itself nonetheless. Is this so different from a wish to tell a person now dead that one loves him?

Imagine that we lived next to a parallel universe. The parallel universe contains people very much like us. We can look into that universe through one-way impenetrable Plexiglas. That is, we can see them, they cannot see us, and we can never enter their world. Now we observe the inhabitants of the parallel universe—the parallels—as they conduct their lives. They have happy and sad occasions, and we rejoice for their good fortunes and pity them for their bad. We might perhaps want to tell one of the parallels how sorry we are for his misfortune, but of course we can't. Were the Plexiglas wall to open up, the motivating force of our emotions might rise to the surface and impel us to action. But until that happens, our emotions might well be motivators though they are presented with no opportunity to motivate.

My claim is that our emotional reactions to fiction might well have motivating force though a motivation that is never exercised because we acknowledge the metaphysical impossibility of interacting with what does not exist. And if this is correct, emotion toward fiction differs from emotion toward actuality not in kind but only in occasion for action. But if there is no difference in kind between emotion toward what is taken to be actual and what is taken to be fictional, then what Charles experiences when his heart palpitates and he grips the arms of his chair is full-fledged, bona fide fear. What else could it be?

Simulating Emotions and Simulated Emotions

The view that the emotions elicited by imaginative interaction with fictional narratives are not full-fledged but only quasi-emotions is the aspect of his theory that has been most strongly resisted. In a recent essay Walton defends the quasi-ness of our emotions toward fiction by recasting make believe as mental simulation.[6]

We are offered the results of an experiment, in which a subject is told that a Mr. Crane and a Mr. Tees are scheduled to take different flights departing at the same time from the same airport, though going to different destinations. Crane and Tees share a cab that is delayed by traffic, and arrive a half-hour after the scheduled departures. Both flights have already left, but Mr. Crane discovers his flight left on time while Mr. Tees learns his flight just left a few minutes ago. Which of the subjects is more upset? Most people think it is Mr. Tees, and they are said to have arrived at this conclusion by simulating the mental attitudes of Tees and Crane.[7]

Alvin Goldman describes such a simulation as imagining "being 'in the shoes' of . . . Tees or Crane. This means pretending to have the same initial desires, beliefs, or other mental states that the attributor's background information suggests the agent has." We then allow those initial states to generate further mental states. "In the case of simulating Tees and Crane, the states are fed into a mechanism that generates an affective state, a state of annoyance or 'upsetness.' More precisely, the output state should be viewed as a pretend or surrogate state, since presumably a simulator doesn't feel the *very same* affect or emotion as a real agent would."[8]

The relevant sense in which emotions induced by imaginative simulations are not the same as those brought on by real experience, according to Walton, is that mental simulations are "imagined or pretend circumstances and states," and the "output" of mental simulations is also a "pretend or surrogate state." The central example of Walton's recent essay asks us to imagine ourselves going deeper and deeper into a cave, whose

6. One of the critics of the view that we don't literally fear (or pity or . . .) fictions is Noël Carroll, *The Philosophy of Horror*, 73–74. The "recent essay" is Kendall Walton's "Spelunking, Simulation, and Slime: On Being Moved by Fiction," in Mette Hjort and Sue Laver, eds., *Emotion and the Arts* (New York: Oxford University Press, 1997).

7. The experiment is by Daniel Kahneman and Amos Tversky, "The Simulation Heuristic," in D. Kahneman, P. Slovic, and A. Tversky, eds., *Judgment Under Uncertainty: Heuristics and Biases* (Cambridge: Cambridge University Press, 1982), 201–7 (as cited by Walton in "Spelunking").

8. Alvin I. Goldman, "Empathy, Mind, and Morals," in Martin Davies and Tony Stone, eds., *Folk Psychology: The Theory of Mind Debate* (Oxford: Blackwell Publishing, 1995), 189 (as cited by Walton in "Spelunking").

passages gradually constrict, until we are forced to stoop, then crawl, then wriggle, until we get stuck and our light goes out. This is said by Walton to be a simulation of spelunking, which propels us into feelings of distress and claustrophobia. But such feelings are "imagined psychological states which the simulator is not actually experiencing."[9]

Not everything that results from a simulated process is itself a simulation. Suppose a car is crashed with test dummies inside. The object is to determine the extent of damage to the car and injuries to its passengers. This counts as a simulation, though what results is real damage to the car (real bashes, real scrapes) but only simulated injuries (simulations, that is, of injuries to real humans).

Walton agrees that a simulation in imagination, if it produces affective responses, might also produce sensations associated with those affects; and if a mental simulation produces such sensations, they would be real. For example, after imagining the spelunking episode, Walton writes, "My shuddering, my clammy palms, my cold sweat, and the sensations that accompany them, are not merely imagined."[10]

But Walton also writes (of the famed Charles and the movie slime): "Charles imagines a Slime oozing toward him, and, in his imagination, it threatens him. It would be strange to deny that he fears it in his imagination also, even were we to decide that his experience counts as one of actually fearing it."[11] To say that Charles fears the slime "in imagination" is to locate his fear ontologically. Now emotion, on a widely accepted analysis, is a quartet of sensation, object, belief, and desire.[12] I tremble with fear over the charging lion because I believe he is dangerous and I don't want to be eaten. Sensation is already admitted by Walton to be real. What remains "in imagination"?

A likely candidate is the object of emotion. The simulator in the sorts of cases that intrigue Walton imagines things that are not factual (oozing slimes, getting stuck in narrow passageways). And if such imaginative simulations generate emotion (fear, anxiety), such emotional response must have objects. One fears the slime or is anxious over being in dark, tight spaces. It may be natural to conclude that the *emotion* is merely simulated because its object is imaginary. I think Walton makes just such an

---

9. Walton, "Spelunking, Simulation, and Slime," 41, 42.

10. Ibid., 41.

11. Ibid., 47.

12. See, for example, Jerome A. Shaffer, "An Assessment of Emotion," *American Philosophical Quarterly* 20 (1983): 161–73.

inference. Regarding someone simulating the experiences of Tees and Crane, Walton writes, "I do not think it is true, literally, that the simulator is *annoyed at having missed her flight*. She *didn't* miss a flight, and she knows it."[13] But it *is* true that the simulator is annoyed at having missed her flight—that is, this truly reports the object of her annoyance. This object is, of course, not real for there is no missed flight. Having missed a flight is, however, the intentional (or phenomenal) object of the simulator's emotion. This object remains only in imagination. But why must we say her *annoyance* is not real annoyance? Suppose I come to believe, wrongly, that I have missed my flight (I'm in a different time zone, say, and have neglected to reset my wristwatch); and on the basis of that false belief, I become annoyed. In truth there is no missed flight, but it seems that I am literally annoyed, even though I am annoyed over nothing real.

Perhaps it is the components of belief or desire that in simulation necessarily remain in imagination. Goldman and Walton's interpretation of the simulation experiment is that I, the simulator, assume the beliefs of Tees and then Crane, and respond accordingly. And because these beliefs are not my own, affective output generated by these beliefs is not my own either, hence is "pretended" or "simulated" (or quasi-) emotion.

But there is something not quite right here. For one thing the potential simulators are told little other than the fact that Tees and Crane are two guys who missed their flights, though Tees's flight just left and Crane's left half an hour ago. What beliefs and desires are we to simulate? Surely we project *ourselves* into their situation and respond as we would. We may be simulating what it would be like to be in Tees's or Crane's situation but we are not simulating what it would be like to be Tees or Crane (for they are, we might say, radically under-developed fictional characters).

Suppose I continue the experiment. In the continuation, I tell you that Mr. Tees goes into the airport bar to wait for the next flight out. A beautiful woman sitting next to him offers to buy him a drink. Now I ask you: Will he accept? The simulationist would advise you to put yourself into his shoes, adopt his beliefs and desires, and see what the output is. But what beliefs and desires will the simulator adopt? If I tell you nothing further, you will either have no answer to give, or will base an answer on what the "typical guy" might do, though the latter is not the result of a simulation but an inductive inference. Suppose I tell you further that Mr. Tees is a single heterosexual guy who dates many women and has no

---

13. Walton, "Spelunking, Simulation, and Slime," 42.

strong commitments, you will of course say that Mr. Tees accepts the drink with pleasure. But again you say this by making an inductive inference from the information given, not by simulating anything.

Indeed, there seem to be insurmountable difficulties in attempting the mental simulation of others' mental states. Some people are genuinely frightened by scary stories to the point of nightmares, and thereby avoid them. I am not that sort of person, but suppose *B* is. Let's suppose that I read a certain novel that has some scary parts, and think *B* may enjoy this novel too. But I caution *B*: you might end up with nightmares. *B* asks me to simulate being the sort of person who is overly frightened by scary stories and then to tell her the output—that is, to tell her whether "I" (that is, I-qua-*B*) would be frightened by this novel. Now I simply cannot do this. *I* am not the sort of person frightened by scary stories, and therefore cannot simulate *B*'s psychological aversions.[14] I can in this case only respond as myself, and I think that what we call "simulation" really amounts to calling up small variations of our own beliefs and desires. And if we "simulate" simply by tweaking our own beliefs and desires a bit, it seems that the emotions thus generated will be our own emotions, hence real ones.

But Walton may disagree. Consider the case, he will urge, where we somehow manage to simulate another's beliefs and desires, and thereby generate emotion. Such an emotion will be itself simulated, hence not really our own, because it is based on beliefs not our own. So that we won't get simulation-by-tweaking, suppose I manage to simulate someone's beliefs and desires quite removed from mine. I make myself believe and want what the Ayatollah Khomeini believed and wanted, and now armed with these beliefs and wants, I generate various affective states such as indignation or fury by looking at women with long uncovered hair or reading Salman Rushdie's *The Satanic Verses*. If I have (and I would say *per impossible*) simulated the beliefs and desires of this orthodox and inflexible cleric to the extent that I bring on feelings of indignation over unveiled women or anger at Rushdie's blasphemies, then it seems that those feelings are the real feelings albeit of a temporary Muslim.

This, however, may not be to the point, which I take to be a defense of the view that emotions toward what we take to be fictions are not fully real or fully our own. Even if I must adopt the beliefs of Mr. Tees to see how "he" would feel about his missed flight, something I have questioned, I rarely adopt the beliefs of fictional characters to see how they

---

14. This echoes a point made by Richard Moran, in "The Expression of Feeling in Imagination," 93.

would respond emotionally. In pitying Anna Karenina, need I adopt *her* beliefs and desires? It suffices that I pity her as I understand her plight, not by "becoming" her and generating emotional output. If I were to see how I would respond were I treated as Anna's husband treats her—for example, asking her to remain in a loveless marriage for the sake of appearance, a request backed up with the threat to cut off contact with her son—I, thus treated, will say I respond with great anger, not the passive acceptance with which Anna responds. (This may be on my part an "intellectual" inference; that is, I need not succeed in *feeling* great anger.) If I miraculously succeed in "becoming" Anna, and succeed also in generating her feelings of passive acceptance, I have generated an emotion not my own. However, this has no bearing on how I pity Anna. *That* feeling requires me to be me, not to become Anna. In sum, simulation won't help Walton's case for the unreality of the quasi-emotions.

emotion with
and without belief

The Factualists and Kendall Walton have lighted on the first proposition (page 8) as the falsehood in the paradox set: Factualists contending that, appearances aside, we do not have emotions toward *fictions*; Walton that we do not, literally, have *emotions* toward fictions. I have argued against both solutions. But now if it is fictions that we have real emotions toward, what is the falsehood in the paradox set? On the theory that I will eventually defend in Chapter 7, it is the second proposition (page 10). The second proposition asserts that any person experiences an emotion— a full-fledged, real emotion—only if he believes that the object of his emotion both exists and exhibits at least some of the emotion inducing properties specific to that emotion. In brief, belief is necessary for emotion. Walton, Radford, and others have endorsed the necessity of belief, and it forms the keystone of the paradox of emotion and fiction. *Is* belief necessary for emotion?

From Feelings to Emotions

What, first of all, is a belief? Someone believes p when he takes p to be true, and disbelieves p when he takes p to be false. Symptoms (though not necessary conditions) that a person believes p include sincerely asserting p, defending the claim that p, objecting when *not-p* is asserted, behaving as if p were true, and the like. Typically, persons have evidence for their beliefs, but one can, without contradiction, believe p without evidence, with insufficient evidence, and even in the face of contrary evidence (evidence for *not-p*). These latter might be called *irrational* beliefs, but beliefs they are nonetheless.

The term "belief" will be the term of choice throughout the remaining discussion, but there are other concepts (at least on many occasions of use) that share with belief the core requirement of taking-to-be-true: one can accept the proposition that p, judge it to be the case that p, be of the opinion that p, and so on. There are, in addition, cognitive attitudes that do not take something to be true and are therefore not beliefs under a different name. One can entertain the thought that p, wonder whether p, suspect p, doubt p, suppose that p, and so on, each without taking p to be true.

On an early theory of emotion, with which it will be instructive to begin, belief is not a constituent of emotion. I'll call this theory "the feeling theory," whose *locus classicus* is *The Emotions* (1922) by William James and C. G. Lange. According to the feeling theory, an emotion is (nothing but) a physical disturbance felt as a pattern of sensation (feeling). Emotions are individuated one from the other according to feel (fear feels one way, shame another, and so on).

Ordinary thinking seems to concur with the feeling theory. At least many people seem to identify the *emotion* of, say, anger, with the *feelings* (sensations, affect) they experience while they are angry, such as pounding heart, a sense of having to maintain self-control, shaky voice, clenched fists, and so on. Of course, anger might give rise to such sensations. The feeling theory asserts that anger *reduces* to (is nothing but) these physical symptoms. Belief is not a necessary part of the feeling theory's picture of emotions, for while belief may trigger patterns of sensation (I believe you to have broken your promise to me and thus feel my blood pressure rise, an impulse to lash out, etc.), the feeling theory holds belief to be external to and thus not a constituent part of the emotion proper. A belief can trigger sensations of anger just as a draft can bring on a sensation of cold, but the belief is no more a constituent part of the anger feelings than the draft is part of the feeling of cold.

But the feeling theory is wrong for two related reasons. First, the feeling theory has difficulty distinguishing between two emotions that have the same raw feel. We may shiver from fear or shiver from anticipation, but there are differences between fear and anticipation that are lost if they are reduced to the shiver. Second, emotion has objects while sensation or mere feeling does not. As one writer puts it, "Emotions are 'odd' because they combine two very different elements of the mental: We feel them as we feel pain, but like thoughts and actions they are directed to or are about things."[1] When sad, we have feelings associated with sadness (perhaps including lethargy, tightness in the chest, and a sensation of oncoming tears), but these sensations come essentially object-directed. We are sad over our dog's death, regret not having gone on the trip, are angry that the car isn't fixed as promised, pity the children whose mother has died, worry that the flood will reach our home, and revere our old professor. Mere feelings (sensations) on the other hand do not take objects. Our headache may be caused by the mechanic's broken promise but the headache (that feeling) is not object-directed in the way that our anger is. A headache is not a headache *that* thus and such is the case. Neither is acid indigestion, blushing (that face-burning sensation), feeling dizzy, feeling like you're about to cry, feeling hungry, feeling a tickle in your throat, and feeling bloated—which is why these are just sensations and not emotions.

Typically, belief or a belief surrogate is brought in to draw the distinctions that we think must be drawn. William Alston, for example, thinks that shame and embarrassment cannot be distinguished on the basis of bodily sensation alone.

> Even if there are in fact subtle differences in the patterns of bodily sensation associated with the two [shame and embarrassment], it seems that what in fact forms the basis of the distinction is that it is necessary for shame but not for embarrassment that the subject take the object to be something which is his fault. . . . And the presence of such evaluations seems to be what makes bodily states and sensations emotional. Some sinkings in the stomach are emotional, because they stem from an evaluation of

---

1. Helen Fay Nissenbaum, *Emotion and Focus* (Stanford: Center for the Study of Language and Information, 1985), 3.

something as dangerous; other sinkings are not emotional because they stem from indigestion.[2]

In Alston's example, we rely on what beliefs we hold to distinguish shame from embarrassment. Jerome Shaffer tells us that we can distinguish admiration and envy only on the basis of belief. Both involve "the belief that the person who is the object of the emotion has some good, but admiration will involve the belief that the person is worthy of it whereas envy will involve the belief that I am worthy of it instead (or, at least, also)."[3] We might also, to take yet another example, need to check our beliefs to distinguish extremes of happiness from extremes of sadness. Since both involve a nearly overwhelming rush of sensation, we might know that we are very happy only when we check our belief that our beloved's life has been spared, not forfeited.

Perhaps the main difficult with the feeling theory is its exclusion of the objects or intentionality of emotion. We do not fear, hope, admire, hate, or pity *simpliciter*. We fear the footsteps behind us in the dark, hope for a cure for AIDS, admire the political activist who works long hours for a goal we think worthy, hate the hypocritical minister who preaches sexual morality and who commits adultery, or pity the homeless whose plight seems so desperate. (The possibility of object-less emotions is examined below.) The sensations of an emotion—fear's heart-racing and stomach-tightening, for example—do not seem, taken by themselves, to be object-directed. But belief has content. I believe that a certain person has been brutally beaten to death. Such a belief might well trigger emotions in me—anger that he has been brutally killed, or pity for his friends—and such a belief can provide the objects of my anger or pity. And if belief is required to provide the object of an emotion, then it would seem that belief is a necessary component of emotion.

The idea that belief is a part of a "complex" that is an emotion is suggested by Shaffer, who claims that an emotion is

> a complex of physiological processes and sensations caused by certain beliefs and desires. . . . To undergo a particular emotion is . . . to undergo a particular kind of physiological and/or sensational state which was caused

---

    2. William Alston, "Emotion and Feeling," *The Encyclopedia of Philosophy*, 8 vols. (New York: Macmillan and The Free Press, 1967), 2:485.
    3. Jerome A. Shaffer, "An Assessment of Emotion." *American Philosophical Quarterly* 20 (1983): 162.

by a particular complex of belief and desire. What emotion it is will be determined by the kind of beliefs and desires and the kind of physiological and sensational effects.[4]

Shaffer thinks emotions to be states necessarily caused by beliefs in the way that a scar is a bit of bodily tissue that by definition is caused by an injury. Thus beliefs (and desires) enter, on Shaffer's view, into the "complex" that is an emotion. I'll take this to be a standard view of emotions.

In one of Shaffer's examples, "I am driving around a curve and see a log across the road. I take it that bodily harm is likely and I don't want that. I turn pale, my heart beats faster, I fell my stomach tighten. I slam on the brakes and stop before I hit the log. I acknowledge that when I saw the log I felt afraid."[5] The "complex" that is my fear, then, consists of this:

> My fear (of hitting the log, of getting injured) is (in the sense of identity) a state caused by my belief that there is a log in the road and that hitting it will probably cause injury and my desire to avoid the log and any injury, and that results in my sensations (turning pale, increased heart rate, stomach tightening).

Shaffer apparently thinks this trio—belief, desire (motive), sensation—to be necessary components of any emotion whatsoever. But he offers little argument beyond presenting what is held up as a paradigm case of emotion and generalizing from it. It is not certain, however, that *every* instance of emotion will contain belief, desire (motive), and sensation. Consider admiration. The paradigm case of admiration might be a state caused by the belief that the admired object has achieved good things in the face of adversity and a sensation of "uplift." However, Kendall Walton thinks that "admiration may seem not always to involve any particularly notable phenomenological experiences at all. There may be a swelling sensation, or a feeling of one's breath being taken away. But there need not be."[6] I myself wonder whether there is any desire or motive associated with anger. Sometimes anger includes the desire that the object of one's anger be "punished" in some way, even a motive to do so oneself; other times anger does not. But the main object of our inquiry is whether belief is necessary. Is belief necessary for any emotion whatsoever, or at least for normal or

4. Ibid., 161.
5. Ibid.
6. Walton, *Mimesis as Make-Believe*, 251.

typical emotions such that its absence makes the emotion seem aberrant or anomalous? If belief is necessary, at least for normal or typical emotions, then Walton's theory of quasi-emotions is at least partially redeemed. We next turn to two proffered counterexamples to the view that belief is necessary for emotion: objectless emotions and the Frances-Fido case.

Objectless Emotions

A constant irritant to the view that belief is necessary for emotion is the suspected existence of objectless emotions: free-floating anxiety, nameless dread, general apathy, worrying over nothing, and the like. If there are objectless emotions—if I can fear without fearing something—then one of the functions of belief, namely, to provide an object for emotion, seems to be uncalled for (though belief may still, for all we know about objectless emotions, still be necessary to trigger them).

Some writers parenthesize objectless emotions, formulating theories around (but not of) them. Irving Thalberg, in a classic essay on emotion, thinks that "depression, euphoria, and total apathy [sometimes] have no objects" as when we "say of someone that he is depressed, euphoric, or apathetic *simpliciter.*" Objectless emotions are "without the concomitance of any beliefs." Thalberg mentions these emotions only to put them aside; he reserves his analysis for any "emotion which has an object," a tactic which permits neater theorizing though one that is suspiciously circular.[7] What are we to make of a view that holds belief to be a necessary condition for those emotions for which belief is a necessary condition?

There are other difficulties with Thalberg's position. So-called objectless emotions may *seem* to be without concomitance of belief, though all this may mean is that the emoter is unable to put his finger on just which beliefs are causing his depression, anxiety, and the like. But it doesn't follow from this that depression or anxiety is not caused by beliefs. Perhaps I believe that my partner no longer loves me, that my colleagues do not value my work, and that my students are bored with my lectures. Yet I don't face up to my beliefs. I end up depressed, though I can't really say why, and my depression seems to me to be free-floating or objectless. I'm

---

7. Irving Thalberg, "Emotion and Thought," originally in *American Philosophical Quarterly* 1 (1964); cited here as reprinted in Stuart Hampshire, ed., *Philosophy of Mind* (New York: Harper & Row, 1966), 205.

not sure if we want to conclude that my depression *is* objectless, for its objects are in all likelihood my believed loss of love, respect, and attention, however unaware I am that I have these beliefs.

In addition, it may well be that an "objectless" frame of mind is not an emotion at all. A person can be happy that he has landed a job. This is an emotion. But a person who wakes up cheery about nothing in particular may not be in an emotional state but in a good *mood*. A person can be anxious over the test results, and this is an emotion. But the anxiety of a person who is anxious over nothing in particular, day after day, seems more like a personality characteristic—like generosity or impetuousness—than an emotional state.

One way, then, to understand objectless "emotions" is as dispositions to react to the world in patterned ways. The cheery person tends to react to most situations along one pattern, the anxious person along another. If such a disposition is temporary it is a mood; if more permanent, a personality type. In neither case must it be an emotion. We call "anxious" both Jack, who is in general anxious, and Jill, who is nervous over taking the test. This not a sheer accident of language for there is a similarity of sensation and behavior. Both Jack and Jill fidget, pace, smoke too much; they each feel tense and agitated. It is in these respects that we call both "anxious." But (so it would seem) until and unless we introduce some sort of *intentional object*, Jack's sensations are on a par with his having taking amphetamines, while Jill's sensations (based on her belief that the test is very important) seem an emotion proper.

Perhaps, then, what we call "objectless emotions" are either moods, or personality traits, or just sensations (mere feelings), but not emotions proper; at the least, "objectless emotions" are not *incontrovertibly* emotions lacking objects. Here's another suggestion: far from taking *no* object, perhaps "free-floating" anxiety or "objectless" cheerfulness take *everything* as its object (a point I owe to Mike McFerren). The free-floatingly anxious person might see everything as somewhat threatening, as the generally euphoric person sees everything as somewhat happy-making. So the anxious person fears the ringing of the telephone; next, he will fear the knock at the door; then, too, he will fear the banging in the pipes; and so on. This is the very opposite of objectless emotion. On such a view, a so-called objectless emotion is an object-directed emotion constantly reiterated though taking different objects each time.

Putative objectless emotions have figured in some attempts at countering Walton's theory. John Morreall has attacked the view that belief is

necessary for emotion. His attack, though, usually concerns the more specific view that a belief in danger is necessary for fear. Morreall disagrees
twice with the second proposition of the paradox set. He thinks, first,
that fear does not always need an intentional object, and consequently
there is not always a need to bring in belief to provide such an object.
And second, Morreall thinks there are ordinary cases of fear without
belief in danger. And if he is correct about fear, then not *all* emotions
require belief.

Morreall thinks there can be objectless fear. "To be frightened by a
loud noise, for example, lower animals and humans need not recognize
the sound as made by a certain kind of thing. . . . When some joker
sneaks up behind us and pops a balloon or shouts 'Boo!' we do not have
to think of a gunshot or rapist to be scared."[8] True, but is the state elicited
by the "Boo" the *emotion* fear? The startle reaction is a sensation, but it
may be no more an *emotional* state than nausea or a sudden stabbing pain
in the neck. We may come to feel the emotion fear *after* the loud noise,
but then we have an object of our fear: an unknown but possibly dangerous threat.

Fiction does sometimes induce mere sensations. There is a moment in
the film *The River Wild* when Merrill Streep's dog, whom we thought
lost, suddenly pops into view on the screen. The audience is startled—
truly startled, not even on Walton's theory quasi-startled—but startled in
exactly the same way that someone looking out his window might be startled by the sudden appearance of a dog popping up unexpectedly. Some
people might experience vertigo when the camera looks down the bell
tower stairs in Alfred Hitchcock's *Vertigo*, a cinematic effect achieved by
physically pulling the camera away while simultaneously zooming the lens
in. But the startle and the vertigo are no more emotions than the nausea
some viewers experience during the scene in *The Tin Drum* in which a
man pulls from the sea a horse's head swarming with live eels.

Morreall thinks that "fear caused by excessive novelty," such as when
children are put to bed in a new house or when an adult assumes a new
job, is "fear without an intentional object."[9] Morreall doesn't allow us to
say that the child is afraid of "the bedroom or the whole house" or that
the adult fears "the new workplace or new life," and for the reason that if
the child or adult were asked if these things are "dangerous" he would be

8. John Morreall, "Fear Without Belief," *Journal of Philosophy* 90 (1993): 361.
9. Ibid., 362.

likely to say "No." This would be convincing if anything we feared *had* to be thought *dangerous* (which Morreall himself doesn't even hold). Suppose we asked instead whether the new bedroom or new job was secure. Now the answer seems likely to be "I'm not sure." Fear of what Morreall calls excessive novelty is fear based not on the belief that the new situation is dangerous but on the belief that it can't yet be trusted. But it is fear based on a belief, and hence fear with an intentional object.

All this worry about objectless emotions, though, is moot because what fiction induces, aside of the sudden appearance of dogs and loud noises, are object-directed emotions. I've tried to cast doubt on the claim that objectless emotions exist. But even if there are, here and there, now and again, objectless emotions, we haven't solved the paradox. *North By Northwest* induces anxiety for Roger Thornhill, not undirected, amorphous, free-floating anxiety. And even if we grant that the startle reaction is fear that is both an emotion and objectless, we will have gotten nowhere regarding Charles whose fear clearly has an object: the approaching slime. And as it stands to this point, it still appears that Charles and his fellow emoters need beliefs to have object-directed emotions, beliefs which Walton among others thinks they do not have.

On Fearing the Harmless

Walton argues that Charles does not believe that the cinematic slime poses a threat and so he cannot really fear it. Morreall wants to show that we can fear something without believing that it is dangerous.[10] His two examples, stage fright and the fear of public speaking, are said to be cases of fear without a belief in danger, though these are unconvincing. People who suffer from such fears are quite likely to believe that they will be thought ridiculous or stupid and fear being humiliated if they stumble or make mistakes. The example of a mother who feels fear for her child as she watches him disappear under a wave though her fear is not based on a belief that *she* is in danger is misplaced, for her fear certainly involves a belief that *her child* is in danger.

And this is the problem with Morreall's putative counterexamples. They may demonstrate that the argument, "Charles doesn't believe himself

10. Ibid., 362ff.

to be in danger, so he can't be really afraid," versions of which Walton deploys several times, is unsound in so far as it depends on the false principle, "Anyone is really afraid only if he believes *himself* to be in danger." But Morreall leaves untouched the larger issue, namely, whether fear (and by extension any emotion) requires a belief of some sort. Walton's argument regarding Charles could be restated without loss of force, "Charles doesn't believe anyone to be in danger, so he can't be really afraid"; and now there is no principle against which Morreall has counterexamples.

Patricia Greenspan presents a perplexing case purporting to dissociate belief from emotion. Frances, once attacked by a rabid dog, genuinely fears all dogs including old Fido, "even though she knows full well that Fido has had his rabies shots and is practically toothless anyway."[11] Frances, it appears, does not believe that Fido is dangerous, for she does not warn others away from him (she lets friends and loved ones play with him). But she herself avoids the dog whenever she can, so it also appears that she genuinely fears him. So what's going on with Frances? Greenspan theorizes as follows:

> Instead of supposing that [Frances's] beliefs come into momentary conflict whenever Fido comes near, it seems simpler, and preferable from the standpoint of rational explanation, to take this as a case where emotion parts from judgment. It exhibits the tendency of emotions, in contrast to a rational agent's beliefs, to spill over to and to fix on objects resembling their appropriate objects in incidental ways.[12]

Greenspan's reading of the case is that Frances fears Fido but her fear "parts from judgment" since she believes there is nothing to be afraid of. This would seem like a neat counterexample to the thesis that belief in some sort of danger is necessary for fear, and by implication counterexample to the thesis that belief is necessary for emotion in general. We get a similar situation from Andrew Solomon, writing of his bout with serious depression, who tells us, "I can remember lying frozen in bed, crying because I was too frightened to take a shower and at the same time knowing that showers are not scary."[13]

11. Patricia Greenspan, "Emotions as Evaluations," *Pacific Philosophical Quarterly* 62 (1981): 158.

12. Patricia Greenspan, *Emotions and Reasons: An Inquiry into Emotional Justification* (New York: Routledge, 1988), 18.

13. Andrew Solomon, "Anatomy of Melancholy," *The New Yorker*, January 12, 1998, p. 48.

Keep in mind that Frances is phobic, Solomon depressed, and it isn't clear that we can generalize from their cases to the norm. Perhaps what Frances's or Solomon's case shows is that in phobic and depressives "emotion parts from judgment"—this may be partly what makes such conditions odd, irrational, or in Solomon's word, ridiculous, and why Walton wants to marginalize the case: "Even if Frances fears in the absence of a belief in danger, this hardly suggests that Charles does."[14]

Yet there are other interpretations of the case. For one, Frances might believe weakly that Fido is harmless but believe more strongly that all dogs are dangerous. This is an inconsistency in her belief scheme, though it does not mean her emotions part company with her judgments exactly, for she acts on the stronger belief, not against *all* judgment.

On the other hand, Frances may be simply behaving very cautiously, though an external observer (Greenspan, for example) takes her to be exhibiting fear. It seems rational, or at least not irrational, to act some-times as if certain things are true even though one doesn't necessarily believe them to be true, and may even have some evidence that they are false. We know it to be false that all guns are loaded and also know it to be false that all wild mushrooms are poisonous. Still a person may handle any gun as if it was loaded, or refuse to eat any wild mushroom as if it were poisonous. Such a person might on occasion even say that a particular wild mushroom is *probably* safe, though still he won't eat it. A person poisoned in the past by a wild mushroom is apt to treat all wild mushrooms with extreme circumspection, though he acknowledges that not all wild mush-rooms are poisonous. This may well be Frances's situation: having been once attacked by a rabid dog, she treats every dog as if dangerous, though she knows that it is false that all dogs are dangerous. On this construal, Frances's caution is at odds with her belief that some dogs are not danger-ous, though her wariness is not at odds with a certain precept she has adopted, namely to treat all dogs cautiously.

Ultimately it isn't clear what conclusion to draw from Frances's fear of Fido, whether it shows that belief is not necessary for fear or whether it shows something else (that Frances is acting on a stronger belief that all dogs are dangerous, or that she is acting not fearfully but cautiously). So the Frances case can't stand as a convincing counterexample to the thesis that belief is necessary for emotion.

14. Walton, *Mimesis as Make-Believe*, 201.

The Sister's Harrowing Tale

Variations on a certain thought experiment percolate through the literature on the paradox. The example seems to occur first in Colin Radford's Aristotelean Society paper,[15] though by the time it makes its way into Noël Carroll's book on horror it has been embroidered into a tale as if by Edward Gorey.

> Imagine that a friend tells you that her sister, a brilliant scientist, has contracted an exotic disease that will kill her within the month. Also, her children, equally brilliant, not to mention well-behaved and full of promise, will be consigned to the care of a cruel and miserly uncle. Undoubtedly, he will put them on a diet of gruel, work the very heart out of them, and discontinue their ballet classes. As catastrophe compounds catastrophe, your consternation mounts. But now imagine that, as soon as you signal an emotional reaction, the friend tells you that she made the whole thing up. She has no sister, there are no children, and there is no gruel. Presumably, the emotion that had been building up dissipates, perhaps to be replaced by another—maybe anger about being gulled.[16]

Commentators on the example from Radford through Carroll think the case shows the necessity of belief for emotion. "What these thought experiments putatively indicate," Carroll writes, "is that there is a necessary bond between our beliefs and our emotions." If the sister's harrowing tale *truly* indicated what it *putatively* indicates, and if the example is a good analogue to fiction, we have a demonstration that belief is necessary for fiction. "Indeed," Carroll remarks, "exactly the same story might be told as a fabrication or marked as a fiction,"[17] in which case we might well feel pity from beginning to end.

Radford used the example, of course, as further demonstration of the irrationality of having emotions toward fictions. Carroll tries to explain away the example's paradoxicality, at least as that example bears on fiction.

> Perhaps it is not the fact that the cock-and-bull story is fabricated that dissipates its reigning emotion, but rather *learning that one has been gulled,*

---

15. Colin Radford, "How Can We Be Moved By The Fate of Anna Karenina?," *Proceedings of the Aristotelian Society*, supp. vol. 49 (1975): 69.

16. Noël Carroll, *The Philosophy of Horror* (New York: Routledge, Chapman and Hall, Inc., 1990), 61.

17. Ibid., 62.

which replaces one emotion with another one, namely resentment or maybe embarrassment. Moreover, since one typically knows that a novel is a fictional fabrication, one does not feel resentful that one has been fooled."[18]

Carroll, in effect, thinks the sister's harrowing tale is not a good analogue to our experience of fiction. In reading *Anna Karenina*, we know from the outset that this is a fiction. We do not unexpectedly encounter at the end the annoying news that there is in actuality no Anna, no adultery, no suffering, no suicide, hence we are not annoyed and continue to pity Anna (at least for a bit longer anyway).

Carroll thinks that resentment drives out—"replaces"—our pity for the sister and that's why our pity vanishes. But why is our pity driven out by resentment rather than coupled with it? After all, we could feel resentment *and* pity. Indeed, the example on its face shows that our pity is eliminated because our belief in the sister's real suffering is eliminated. Carroll's explanation simply finesses the role of belief in generating our original feelings of pity. As someone who adopts a thought theory (on which see the following chapters) Carroll must show that belief (or taking true) is not necessary for emotion, despite what the sister's harrowing tale "putatively indicates." And this he hasn't done. I suspect that if we get clearer on what's going on in the sister's tale, we will have a solution to the paradox within grasp.

Suppose belief and emotion regularly (I do not say invariably) occur together. It follows that there is some causal relation between belief and emotion. Next, take away belief and, lo, the emotion dissipates. What follows now? Either that belief is causally necessary for emotion or that belief is causally sufficient for emotion. It does not follow that belief is necessary for emotion. To prove that, we need further data. But I want to argue that the sister's tale, given some additional assumptions, proves at most that belief is causally sufficient for emotion.

Let's engage in another thought experiment, one that will have the same structure as the sister's harrowing tale. In this experiment you place an airtight clear glass bell jar over a lighted candle. Rather quickly, the candle's flame goes out. Apparently, then, fire goes on in the presence of oxygen, and goes out when oxygen is removed. Does the experiment demonstrate that oxygen is *necessary* for fire? No. For all the experiment tells us, there

18. Ibid., 77.

could be an as yet unknown substance, call it for the moment "smoxygen," in the presence of which fire will burn, just as it does in the presence of oxygen. Indeed, suppose we now search for smoxygen and discover that there really is such a substance. That is, there is a gas, chemically different from oxygen, that allows fire to burn just as if oxygen were part of the process. Suppose we have a sensing device that will tell us if we are in the presence of oxygen or smoxygen. We now conduct an additional experiment. We empty a chamber of oxygen, fill it with smoxygen (verified by our sensing device), light a candle, observe its flame, cover it with a bell jar, and observe the flame go out. Clearly, neither oxygen nor smoxygen is individually *necessary* for fire, though we can now conclude that either smoxygen or oxygen is individually sufficient for fire.

We are speaking, of course, of causal, not logical, sufficiency (that is, sufficiency in the actual world, not in all possible worlds). A causally sufficient condition can be either what I'll call a starter or a continuer. A *starter* is a condition C that is causally sufficient for another condition D, yet C does not need to continue to exert causal force for D to maintain itself. When a cue ball hits an eight ball and sends the latter in a certain direction, the cue ball is a starter for the eight ball. The cue ball need not continue to exert any further influence on the eight ball for the latter to continue in its path. Indeed, the cue ball can strike the eight ball and then be removed immediately from the table. The eight ball will continue in the same path regardless. Other causally sufficient conditions are continuers. A *continuer* provides a sufficient condition for some process to continue, not by starting that process but by being present and entering into the process during its duration.

To put this jargon to use in the candle thought experiment: at first we note that oxygen is a continuer for the candle to burn. (Oxygen isn't a starter; the match is.) It was tempting initially to think that oxygen to be the *only* continuer around for flame—tempting, that is, to think oxygen to be a *necessary* continuer for flame. But our discovery of smoxygen disproves this. Smoxygen is another continuer for flame. Hence oxygen, while perhaps far more prevalent than smoxygen, isn't necessary for combustion at all.

The sister's harrowing tale is very much like the original candle experiment. The tale shows *something* about the relation of belief to emotion, though in itself it is inconclusive as to whether belief is sufficient or necessary for emotion (or both). We need further data. Suppose we suspect that another kind of mental state, one different from belief, can engender emotion. We harbor this suspicion largely because we observe people having emotions while reading or watching works they know to be fictional. Call this nonbelief mental state "thought." Both thought and belief involve considering propositions, though thought simply entertains a proposition while belief takes it to be true. Now if thought *or* belief can bring on emotion, we will conclude that belief is causally sufficient though not necessary for emotion.

It would further seem that thought or belief functions as a continuer rather than a starter. It is the friend's telling of her sister's harrowing tale that starts the pity. It is our belief that the tale is true—that the sister must be suffering this or that—which continues our pity. And our pity can, and probably would, go on, continued by belief, after the tale is told and done—that is, if we weren't informed that the whole tale was made up. When belief is thus eliminated, it is like putting a bell jar over the candle flame. The only continuer sufficient for the process is thereby removed, and the process is extinguished as well.

Suppose we continue the experiment involving the sister's tale. "Calm down," your friend tells you, "I'm sorry I bamboozled you that way. But you must admit it's a heart-rending tale nonetheless. Let me tell it again." And she does—as it happens she is a master storyteller—only this time you entertain the harrowing tale in thought. This is like doing the candle experiment a second time, using smoxygen without oxygen. If you end up feeling pity during the re-telling when the tale is told openly as fiction you feel your pity without the presence of belief though in the presence of certain thoughts concerning the sister and her plight. Why then did you lose your pity when you were told that the harrowing tale was an untruth? Not because anger drove it away but because belief is a continuer for emotion, and that continuer was removed with no replacement. Why can you feel pity in the second, openly fictional, retelling? Because now there is another continuer for the emotion, which we'll call for the moment "thought."

Suspicion and Other Nonbeliefs

Can thoughts that are not taken to be true cause emotion? Neither Morreall's nor Greenspan's cases convincingly indict proposition 2 of the paradox set, though for all the tenacity with which solvers of the paradox cling to the necessity of belief for emotion, cases of emotion generated by something other than belief turn out to be fairly common.

CASE 1. Ted suspects that he is late for a dinner party.[19] He's on his way, expecting to arrive about eight o'clock, perhaps a few minutes after. Still, he has a nagging feeling. He isn't sure he has the time right. He thinks he was invited for eight, but could it be seven? And he begins to feel anxious over being late. If we ask him whether he believes (thinks it true) that he's late, Ted will say, "Well, no, not exactly. I'm just not sure I have the time right. I really should have called the host earlier to see what time I'm expected. But I didn't, and as it is I'll just have to hope I'm not late. It's a very important party."

CASE 2. Jill is waiting for news of her lover, Jack. Jack has gone mountain climbing in Exland, a country where several Americans have been recently killed, apparently for political reasons. Now Jack did not show up for his return flight, and in fact hasn't been heard from for some days. Jill is in a state of high anxiety; and though she doesn't believe Jack to be dead, she doubts that he is safe and sound. And because Jill doubts that Jack is safe, she is quite fearful.

CASE 3. "Standing on a precipice," Noël Carroll writes, "one might fleetingly entertain the thought of falling over the edge. Commonly, this can be accompanied by a sudden chill or a tremor which is brought about . . . not by our belief that we are about to fall . . . but by our thought of falling. . . . Moreover, we are not frightened by the *event* of our thinking of falling, but by the *content* of our thought of falling—perhaps the mental image of plummeting through space."[20] Our thought of falling is certainly not a belief that we are falling, nor a belief that we will fall. Yet because of our thought we feel suddenly afraid.

CASE 4. Sigmund Freud's essay, "The Relation of the Poet to Day-Dreaming," gives a nicely crafted example of how fantasy generates emotion.

> Take the case of a poor orphan lad, to whom you have given the address of some employer where he may perhaps get work. On the way there he falls into a day-dream suitable to the situation from which it springs. The content of the phantasy will be somewhat as follows: He is taken on and pleases his new employer, makes himself indispensable in the business, is taken into the family of the employer, and marries the charming daughter

---

19. This is a variation of a case suggested by Mike McFerren, though Irving Thalberg in "Emotion and Thought" also has examples of emotion caused by suspicions, doubts, and hopes.

20. Carroll, *Philosophy of Horror*, 80.

of the house. Then he comes to conduct the business, first as a partner, and then as successor to his father-in-law.[21]

Freud wants to use this case as entry into the wellsprings of the poet's material (which ultimately is wish as expressed in fiction, or so Freud thought). But his case serves our purposes as well. Suppose we continue Freud's case in a very plausible way. The orphan lad as a result of his day-dream becomes elated. We might say that he is elated because in thought he gets the job. Now we have elation without belief.

As I have told these stories, neither Ted, nor Jill, nor the person on the precipice, nor the orphan lad takes the thought that generates their emo-tion to be true; hence none of them believes it. Lest this be considered question-begging, let us consider the possibility that Ted, Jill, the man on the precipice, and the orphan lad have, somehow and briefly, taken some-thing to be true: Ted momentarily believes that he really is late, Jill that her lover has been assassinated by political terrorists, the man on the precipice that he really is about to fall, the orphan lad that he has indeed landed the job, married the boss's daughter, and become head of the firm. Further, it is at (or just after) the point when belief is evinced that the pro-tagonist begins to feel emotion.

It would seem that someone could move from not believing *p* to believing *p* only if there is a change either in the evidence in his possession or the weight he assigns it. Call his evidence as he weighs it a person's doxastic entitlement. I may take it to be true at *t* that the butler murdered the cook with a gun in the pantry only to change my mind a moment later when I am told (or recall) that the butler was on the telephone in the parlor when the shot rang out. My doxastic entitlement changed (and it may change again if I later decide that the evidence that the butler was on the telephone in the parlor is itself not terribly credible—perhaps I took it to be true solely because the butler himself told me!).

But there is no change in any of the doxastic entitlement of the main characters in the preceding four examples. Ted isn't filled with apprehen-sion because he decided to check his appointment book only to find *Din-ner at 7* plainly staring out at him and now knows he is late. Jill hasn't been given another scrap of information which tips her evidential scales so that she now *believes* that persons unknown have done in the Jack. The

21. Sigmund Freud, "The Relation of the Poet to Day-Dreaming" (1908), as reprinted in a collection of Freud's essays assembled by Benjamin Nelson, *On Creativity and the Unconscious* (New York: Harper & Row, Inc., 1958), 49.

man standing on the edge of the precipice need not abruptly *believe* his situation has become more precarious, as he might if, for example, the ground began to tremble. The orphan lad has not, just before his fantasy, precipitately taken his getting an interview as good evidence that a word has been put in for him with the prospective employer, so that he now *believes* that he will get the job, his "fantasy" being merely an inductive drawing out of the implications of the evidence. It's not that such examples couldn't be generated. The point is that they aren't the four cases I've described. In those cases, someone begins to emote—but not because they've come to a point where they *believe* something.

On the standard view, belief has been thought of as a necessary constituent of emotion, and this because belief was thought necessary to trigger emotions, to individuate emotions, and to provide the objects of emotions. Jane is elated. Why is she elated? Because she believes that she has been admitted to a superb medical school, her admission being at the same time the object of her elation. But other mental states can serve the same function. Ted is anxious. Why is Ted anxious and what is the object of his anxiety? Ted is anxious because he suspects he is late for an important social function, and his lateness is the object of his anxiety. Jill is fearful because she doubts that Jack is safe. The object of her fear is that Jack is harmed. The orphan lad is elated because he entertains the thought that he will get the job and marry the boss's daughter, this thought being both cause and object of his elation. Suspicion, doubt, and thinking something possible can perform the same functions as belief with respect to individuating emotions and providing their objects.

Belief, then, is really not necessary for emotion. However, we haven't quite crossed the threshold into fiction yet. For each of the four cases have an existential component for the emoter. Ted, Jill, and the rest assume that there *exists* something (a dinner party, a man missing in a foreign country, a precipice, a job) though they may not *believe* something of this existent object. Ordinary emoters toward fiction do not have this existential component. This is why the four examples, though examples of emotion generated without benefit of belief, are not exact analogues to our experience of fiction. For no one reading *Anna Karenina* even as much as suspects that there is an Anna Karenina suffering what is described in the novel.

In fact, the stress on *belief* in discussions of the paradox is misleading. The four cases I've described show how emotion can be generated in the absence of belief, though they are not examples of emotion generated in the absence of existential commitment. The apparentness of proposition 2 rests as much on belief as on existential commitment. Factualism and Counterfactualism (especially of the were-any-of-my-friends-in-Anna's-shoes variety) can be seen as attempts to provide an existential component to our experience of fiction. But in truth our experience of fiction is an experience of what is believed at some level not to exist.

When the typical emoter thinks that Roger Thornhill is in danger from the flying crop duster, this thought causing him anxiety, he not only does not believe Roger Thornhill is in danger, he does not believe there is any Roger Thornhill at all. This makes the case of the emoter toward fiction unlike those of the other four, who generate emotion from cognitive states that are not beliefs but at least assert the existence of their objects. How can thought theory even get off the ground?

six

thought theory
from coleridge
to lamarque

"Thought theory" is the name Noël Carroll has given to a class of theories whose central contentions are (a) belief is not necessary for emotion, and (b) imagining something (just thinking it, though not thinking it true) frequently sparks emotion in the imaginer. When thought theorists address the issue, most also put forward (c) the emotions inspired by imagination are real, not quasi, emotions (the one exception is Roger Scruton in whose theory imagination generates attenuated feelings he calls "aesthetic emotions").

Kendall Walton, of course, has the player of a game of make-believe imagine (entertain, consider, turn over in his mind) certain things, but games of make-believe involve more. Someone who plays a game of make-believe using, say, Hitchcock's *Rebecca* as a prop imagines not just that Mrs. Danvers, the housekeeper, is tempting the new Mrs. de Winter to drown herself in the sea but also imagines of himself that he is witness to Mrs. Danvers intimate and destructive conversation with the new mistress of Manderlay. Thought theory runs on the structurally simpler activity of imagining that Mrs. Danvers is trying to get the new Mrs. de Winter to drown herself. The two theories differ in emphasis. I think it correct to say that for Walton it is the *activity* of playing games of make-believe that is the primary causal force in generating (quasi-) emotion, though of course the content of what is imagined determines what (quasi-) emotion, if any, we feel. On thought theory, the *content* of what we imagine is what is most responsible for the emotion we feel, the act of imagining being mainly a way of bring content before the mind's eye.

I have argued in Chapter 4 that the apparatus of games of make-believe, even supplemented with the mechanism of simulation, does not entail that the affective results of such games (or simulations) will be anything but full-fledged emotion. But now it is time to make a declaration. I simply do not find myself playing Waltonian games of make-believe when I read novels, view movies, and attend plays. I particularly resist the implication that I become (fictional) participant in the drama, (fictionally) lurking just out of camera range as Mrs. Danvers talks to the shy and troubled Mrs. de Winter in Rebecca's bedroom. (Since neither of the fictional participants to that conversation ever notice me I must be *especially* fictional.) The idea of imagination *de se* as Walton deploys it strikes me as false to my experience, mainly because I think my reactions to works of fiction are more voyeuristic than participatory; and here, I think, my intuitions simply clash with Walton's, who writes, "Participants in games of make-believe need to be distinguished from mere onlookers."[1] I think we *are* mere onlookers to "fictional worlds." The analogy with our appreciation of fictions is not playing a game in which stumps are bears but peering through a window at the people and situations inside.

There is a logical point beside this clash of intuitions and claims of how it is to me. If two theories can, potentially, explain the phenomenon of emotion toward fiction, though one theory is simpler, then the law of parsimony (Ockham's Razor, if you like) would pick the simpler. Thus thought theory, if it can explain emotion toward fiction, should on grounds of simplicity if nothing else be the correct theory.

Among those advocating some version of thought theory are Samuel Taylor Coleridge, Roger Scruton, David Novitz, Peter Lamarque, Noël

---

1. Kendall Walton, *Mimesis as Make-Believe* (Cambridge: Harvard University Press, 1990), 209.

Carroll, Susan Feagin, and eventually, in the next chapter, myself.[2] These advocates cling to thought theory's central tenets but disagree on other matters. In this chapter, I examine three thought theories with an eye toward extracting what works in them as well as avoiding their mistakes. There are several key questions I put to any thought theory.

- How does the theory handle the emoter's disbelief in the reality of the objects of his emotion? And how will such disbelief not nip any emotion in the bud?
- What are the thoughts that generate emotion? Must they replicate the fictional propositions of the narrative? Are such thoughts invariably propositional?
- How do thoughts act? What "causal dynamism" in Bijoy Boruah's phrase do they have to bring on emotion?[3] When do they fail to bring on emotion?
- Are the emotions produced ordinary or extraordinary?

That Willing Suspension of Disbelief

This phrase, which inevitably comes to mind when discussing the paradox, is of course from Samuel Taylor Coleridge, who is nearly alone among pre–twentieth-century theorists in seeing the paradox of emotion and fiction, and is the first thought theorist. In *Biographia Literaria*, Coleridge describes the original plan of the *Lyrical Ballades* he was to write with William Wordsworth,

> in which it was agreed, that my endeavors should be directed to persons and characters supernatural, at least romantic; yet so as to transfer from

2. Samuel Taylor Coleridge, *Biographia Literaria*, chap. 14, from *The Collected Works of Samuel Taylor Coleridge*, ed. James Engell and W. Jackson Blaine (Princeton: Princeton University Press for the Bollingen Foundation, 1983), vol. 7, pt. 2; Roger Scruton, *Art and Imagination: A Study in the Philosophy of Mind* (London: Methuen & Co. Ltd, 1974; corrected edition, London: Routledge & Kegan Paul Ltd, 1982); David Novitz, "Fiction, Imagination and Emotion," *Journal of Aesthetics and Art Criticism* 38 (1980): 279–88; Peter Lamarque, "How Can We Fear and Pity Fictions?," *British Journal of Aesthetics* 21 (1981): 291–304; Noël Carroll, *The Philosophy of Horror* (New York: Routledge, 1990), chap. 2; Susan L. Feagin, *Reading With Feeling* (Ithaca: Cornell University Press, 1996).

3. Bijoy Boruah, *Fiction and Emotion: A Study in Aesthetics and the Philosophy of Mind* (Oxford: Clarendon Press, 1988), 92–93.

our inward nature a human interest and a semblance of truth sufficient to procure for these shadows of imagination that willing suspension of disbelief for the moment that constitutes poetic faith.[4]

In a letter, Coleridge described at some further length just how "poetic faith" could be achieved.

Images and Thoughts possess a power in and of themselves, independent of that act of the Judgement or Understanding by which we affirm or deny the existence of a reality correspondent to them. Such is the ordinary state of the mind in Dreams. It is not strictly accurate to say, that we believe our dreams to be actual while we are dreaming. We neither believe it or disbelieve it—with the will the comparing power is suspended, and without the comparing power any act of Judgement, whether affirmation or denial, is impossible. The Forms and Thoughts act merely by their own inherent power: and the strong feelings at times apparently connected with them are in point of fact bodily sensations, which are the causes or occasions of the Images, not (as when we are awake) the effects of them. Add to this a voluntary Lending of the Will to this suspension of one of it's [*sic*] own operations (i.e. that of comparison & consequent decision concerning the reality of any sensuous Impression) and you have the true Theory of Stage Illusion— equally distant from the absurd notion of the French Critics, who ground their principles on the presumption of an absolute *De*lusion, and of Dr Johnson who would persuade us that our Judgements are as broad awake during the most masterly representation of the deepest scenes of Othello, as a philosopher would be during the exhibition of a Magic Lanthorn.[5]

What makes him a thought theorist is Coleridge's contention that "images and thoughts" possess a "power" independent of "judgment or understanding" (independent of belief), a power sufficiently strong to bring on "strong feelings" (though these are said to be "bodily sensations"—mere quasi-emotions?). It is all but indisputable that thought alone can bring on emotion. The parent whose child is late coming home from school and who entertains thoughts of traffic accidents or kidnapping can bring on feelings of anxiety and dread. "Think of a vomit sandwich," Susan Feagin enjoins, and you will feel disgust even though for all

---

4. Coleridge, *Biographia Literaria*, chap. 14, from *Collected Works*, vol. 7, pt. 2, p. 6.
5. Letter to Daniel Stuart of May 13, 1816, as quoted in Coleridge's *Collected Works*, vol. 7, pt. 2, p. 6, n. 2.

you know no such thing is or ever was.[6] Now there are, of course, unresolved questions here, not the least of which is how we are to understand the "inherent power" of images and thoughts to bring on emotion. Coleridge, however, never addresses that question for the topic of his letter is the suspension of disbelief.

Samuel Johnson had addressed the "impossibility" a spectator is supposed to find in a Shakespeare play when in the first act he is "at Alexandria" and in the second "at Rome, at a distance to which not the dragons of Medea could, in so short a time, have transported him." But there is really no impossibility here. "The truth is," Johnson wrote, "that the spectators are always in their senses, and know, for the first act to the last, that the stage is only a stage, and that the players are only players."[7]

Coleridge's response to Johnson is that when we are immersed in the story we are like a dreamer who lacks the power to judge his dreams as true or false, hence who neither believes or disbelieves his dreams. Thus Coleridge understands the *suspension* of disbelief to imply a *paralysis* of the power of judgment. But one who takes a character to be fictional has *already* rendered a judgment. Even if a spectator's power of judgment were at the time he is watching *Anthony and Cleopatra* somehow paralyzed (which it is not), this would only render such a spectator incapable of making further judgments, though it would not hide from the spectator his disbelief in the actuality of the characters on stage. In any case, the theory that spectators to plays are like dreamers who *can't* verify what parades before their mind's eye seems simply wrong (as does the suggestions that a dreamer neither believes nor disbelieves his dreams—no less an authority than Descartes takes dreams as occasions for deception, which can only imply that the dreamer *does* believe his dreams).

A contemporary thought theorist, David Novitz, writes of the "statements" of *The Pickwick Papers* that "it is as misguided to believe them as it is to disbelieve them."[8] Novitz does not imply an inability to believe or disbelieve the statements of fiction; rather he suggests that it is a mistake to do so. However, this puts the reader of *Pickwick Papers* in the position of a judge who thinks it wrong (because it would bias him) to believe or disbelieve plaintiff's testimony until he has heard from all parties. But

---

6. Feagin, *Reading With Feeling*, 139. In a footnote, Feagin attributes the example to Howard Niblock.

7. Samuel Johnson, "Preface to *Shakespeare*," in Hazard Adams, ed., *Critical Theory Since Plato* (New York: Harcourt Brace Jovanovich, 1971), 335.

8. Novitz, "Fiction, Imagination and Emotion," 281.

appreciators of fiction do not have bias to worry about. Or it puts the reader in the position of an agnostic who thinks he has equal evidence for and against the existence of God, and that it would be wrong (on grounds of rationality) to believe or disbelieve in God's existence since there is no better evidence for one over the other. But there is not equally weighty evidence both for and against Mr. Pickwick's actuality, and no reason from rationality to withhold disbelief in Pickwick's actuality.

The error these thought theorists fall into is to understand the *suspension* of disbelief as its *abolition*. If Dr. Johnson was wrong in having our "judgments" be "broad awake" during *Othello*, Coleridge and Novitz are equally wrong in banishing them altogether.

Unasserted Emotions

Roger Scruton's book *Art and Imagination* raises the paradox of emotion and fiction *en passant*, when he discusses an example of fearing an enraged lion in a picture by Delacroix. Scruton's leading question is not How can we pity Anna Karenina?, but rather How shall we characterize the experience of finding a piece of music to be sad? This latter question is sometimes re-asked as How shall we characterize the aesthetic emotions, for example, aesthetic sadness? What we are said to feel before the picture of the enraged lion is aesthetic fear. Generalizing, then, any emotion engendered in us by a fiction will be of the aesthetic variety. What, now, is an aesthetic emotion? The answer is said to be found in considerations of the imagination especially as it stands in contrast with belief.[9] The imagination is supposed to be the paradigm of a noncognitive mental state, as belief is the paradigm of cognitive mental activity. What is the difference between the two?

Both belief and imagination are language-dependent to this extent: In order to refer to those propositions a person believes or imagines we must "mention the declarative sentences that express them."[10] However, since we can think that p, suppose that p, entertain the possibility that p, and the like without thereby believing that p, belief must involve something more than a declarative sentence held in the head ("before the mind").

9. Scruton, *Art and Imagination*, chap. 6.
10. Ibid., 87.

Assertion turns out to be the key to this something more.[11] In Scruton's view, to believe that p is to have a disposition to assert that p, while to judge that p is to assert on a particular occasion that p.[12] In contrast, there are the unasserted propositions that one may from time to time entertain, suppose, think about, and the like.

> In these acts [entertaining, supposing, and the rest] propositions come before one's mind, and it seems to be a necessary consequence of the way in which this idea of an unasserted thought has been introduced that what is before one's mind in entertaining p is precisely what is asserted in assert-ing p, and hence precisely what is believed in believing p. Thus when we imagine something, or tell a story, while being indifferent to its truth, the content of our thought is the content of a belief; but the thought process itself is independent of this belief.[13]

In believing p we are disposed to assert (judge) that p, though Scruton will sometimes truncate this and say that in believing that p we hold the *asserted* thought that p. In merely imagining that p we are not disposed to assert that p, though here again Scruton will say that in imagining that p we hold the *un*asserted thought that p. To hold the unasserted thought that p is (Scruton says) to be indifferent to the truth of p, and presumably the opposite holds of believing that p: then we are precisely *not* indiffer-ent to the truth of what we believe. More is required for imagining (that) p other than simply holding p in mind unasserted.[14] But we need not go into these further conditions to get to Scruton's views on aesthetic emo-tions, which trade on mainly on their "unasserted" character.

11. Scruton acknowledges this idea to Peter Geach's *Mental Acts* (London, 1957) and Bruce Aune's *Knowledge, Mind and Nature* (New York, 1967), though it has its roots in Gottlob Frege's essay "Sense and Reference," which can be found in *Translations from the Philosophical Writings of Gottlob Frege*, 2d ed., trans. and ed. Peter Geach and Max Black (Oxford: Blackwell, 1966).

12. At least I take this to be Scruton's view. What he says is this: "Geach [Scruton tells us] has argued that judging that p is a mental act analogous to the overt act of asserting 'p'. Now, believing and judging are different concepts. . . . Believing, unlike judging, is dispositional or quasi-dispositional: it is not a mental occurrence of the same instantaneous variety. But this should not worry us unduly, since everything that we need to say about the contrast between belief and other modes of thought can be expressed in terms of the contrast between judgement and other kinds of mental act" (*Art and Imagination*, 88).

13. Ibid., 89.

14. For example, we must in imagining that p go "beyond what is given in ordinary belief" (Ibid., 98), i.e., one must add "one's own invention" (100). Also, "imagining is a special case of 'thinking of x as y,'" but imagination does not simply produce descriptions—this would be mere "fantasy or whim"; one constructs descriptions that are "appropriate" (98). See also the discussion of "seeing" and "seeing as" (107ff.).

In the first place, aesthetic emotions are generated not by beliefs but by imaginings.

> We might say—simplifying somewhat—that an emotion is, normally, a complex of belief and desire, united in a causal relation. But aesthetic emotions are not founded on belief but rather on the entertaining of propositions unasserted. Before an enraged lion I feel fear, and my fear is on a piece with the awareness of a dangerous object. But before a lion hunt by Rubens or Delacroix I have no such awareness: the propositions that I entertain about the dangerous object are not asserted.[15]

In the case of a real lion hunt, I would have certain beliefs, for example, the belief that I was in the presence of a lion, and I would also have certain desires, such as the "desire that the danger should be removed and the lion's ferocity overcome."[16] In regarding a painting of a lion hunt, however, I merely believe myself to be in the presence of a certain painting and experience a desire to look at it. *Pari passu* with unasserted thoughts, an aesthetic emotion will have "content" without "assertion." What counts as content and assertion for emotions?

> [S]uppose we were to characterize fear: we refer to the beliefs, the desires, the "passive" symptoms such as trembling, sweating and palpitating, and the causal relations that bind all these together. And suppose we propose this (as would be correct) as a complete analysis of fear. . . . And if we subtract from this description those elements that are expressions of the beliefs and desires characteristic of "real" fear, then there is no reason to think that we have not given a full characterization, in what remains, of the symptoms of "imagined" fear.[17]

The "content" of an emotion, then, is its "passive" (physical) symptoms. To "assert" the emotion would be to have desires toward action, and it is precisely this "assertive" character that aesthetic emotions lack. Scruton also denies that "the subject's emotion before the painted lion hunt has the same intensity as the corresponding 'real' or 'factual' emotion."[18] In summary:

15. Ibid., 129.
16. Ibid.
17. Ibid., 131–32.
18. Ibid., 129.

Scruton's View

Real fear of an enraged lion:	Aesthetic fear of an enraged lion:
Believing (taking it to be true) that there is an enraged lion about to attack.	Imagining that (being indifferent to the truth of) there is an enraged lion about to attack.
which typically produces	*which typically produces*
The "passive symptoms" of fear (trembling, palpitations, etc.).	The "passive symptoms" of fear (trembling, palpitations, etc.), though symptoms of lesser intensity than those of real fear
and	*and nothing further.*
Desires (for example, wanting to flee, to shoot the lion, etc.).	

Scruton makes four important claims about aesthetic emotions. First, aesthetic emotions result because of our supposed indifference to the truth of what we imagine. Second, such imaginings have sufficient causal power to produce aesthetic emotion. Third, aesthetic emotions are less intense than real emotions. And fourth, real emotion always invokes an impetus to act, but aesthetic emotion never does. I've already argued against the fourth claim in the chapter on Walton. I'll focus here on the other three.

First, Scruton claims that to imagine that p is to hold the "unasserted thought" that p, which Scruton instructs us to understand as "being indifferent to the truth of p"—shades of the suspension of disbelief. But again there is something not right. In looking at a painting that depicts a charging lion, I may do something like entertain the thought (or imagine) that a lion is charging, but I am hardly *indifferent* to the truth of this thought. Far from it! The fact that I know (on some level) that I stand before a painted lion—that I know (on some level) that the proposition "There is a real lion charging me now" is false—must play an essential role in explaining why I am not inclined to flee, to shoot, to scream, and so on.

Second, regarding Boruah's problem of causal dynamism: We need some state or event, presumably mental, which has sufficient causal force to generate an emotion. Belief in the normal (nonfiction) case is the causal dynamo that begets emotion. My belief that a lion is charging me is the principal causal force that causes me to feel fear (and attempt to flee). What causal powers are there in imagination—in holding the unasserted thought that there is a lion about to charge? Scruton's implied answer is that aesthetic emotion is less intense than real emotion (i.e., emotion generated by imagination is less intense than emotion generated by belief). If imagination produces a weakened form of emotion than such emotion requires less causal force than real emotion. Now it is nearly incontrovertible that I will feel less fear (if indeed I feel any fear) observing a painting of a charging lion than what I will feel catching sight of a real lion charging. However, the point is more general. Scruton's theory predicts that I will feel less pity for fictional characters than for real people. But there would seem to be counterexamples to this. It is not improbable—maybe even likely—that a person reading Tolstoy's novel will feel more intensely for Anna Karenina (whom he takes to be fictional) than for a real woman whose plight resembles Anna's and which he has read about in the morning's paper. Even if we have a theory of how it is that imagination generates emotion, it will not be a theory that is able to rely on a lessened form of emotion.

Thoughts and Their Contents

Perhaps the best known contemporary exponent of thought theory is Peter Lamarque, who asked, "What are we responding *to* when we fear Othello and pity Desdemona?" and answered, "It is my contention that the real objects of our fear in fictional cases are thoughts. We are frightened *by* thoughts, though we are not frightened *of* thoughts."[19] Thoughts, according to Lamarque, can be propositional or predicative.

> The thought that-the-moon-is-made-of-green-cheese has a content identified under a propositional description, the thought a-piece-of-cheese is identified under a predicative description. By allowing both types of descriptions I intend to admit as thoughts everything we might consider as mental contents, including mental images, imaginings, fantasies, suppositions, and all that Descartes called "ideas."[20]

19. Peter Lamarque, "How Can We Fear and Pity Fictions?," 294.
20. Ibid., 293.

It is thoughts generated by encounters with works of fiction that move us to emotion. "We can be frightened by the thought of something without believing that there is anything real corresponding to the content of the thought. At most we must simply believe that the thought is frightening."[21]

Further, "The fear associated with a frightening thought is a genuine, not a 'quasi' or fictional fear." How is it we can be "frightened by thoughts"? It is here that Lamarque can be seen as giving a further account of what Coleridge referred to as the "inherent power" of thought to cause emotion. "The propensity of a thought to be frightening is likely to increase in relation to the level of reflection or imaginative involvement that is directed to it."[22] These levels of "reflection" and "involvement" reduce to the "vividness" of a thought and the "level of attention we give to it." The idea is that the more vivid a thought and the more we attend to it, the greater chance it has of bringing on an emotional state. Lamarque's suggestion is on the right track, and I'll return to and defend vividness and attentiveness in the following chapter. I want here to take up and dispose of another issue.

Lamarque attempts to connect our thoughts with the work of fiction. "What thought-contents must we be responding to for us truly to be said to be fearing Othello or pitying Desdemona?" Lamarque asked. "Not any tears are tears for Desdemona, not any thoughts are thoughts about Othello. Strict criteria must be applied to identify the right thoughts and thus the right tears." To have thoughts about Desdemona we must somehow trace our thoughts back to Shakespeare's play. The "paradigm connection" Lamarque thinks "would be one of *identity of content* where the very propositions or predicates expressed by Shakespeare also identify our thoughts." More specifically, the paradigm is to be moved by thoughts "which are identified through the descriptive or propositional content *either* of sentences in the fiction *or* of sentences logically derived from the fiction *or* of sentences supplementing the sentences of the fiction in appropriate ways." These "sentences supplementing the sentences of the fiction in appropriate ways" result from a kind of deep interpretation of the fiction "as when we say, for example, that *Othello* is about Machiavellian sophistication and the destruction of innocence." Such interpretations, Lamarque says, may "in turn evince further emotions."[23]

21. Ibid., 294.
22. Ibid., 295.
23. Ibid., 300–303.

For example, Shakespeare writes that Desdemona does not have the handkerchief Othello had given her and strongly implies, though he does not state, that Desdemona is innocent of adultery with Cassio, which would, I think, count as a logical derivation from the fiction, though an inductive, not a deductive, derivation. We might, with Stanley Cavell, interpret Othello's strange trust in Iago and precipitous rage at Desdemona as evidence that Othello tries against his knowledge of Desdemona's innocence to believe Iago, and this because Othello needs to deny Desdemona's surprising passion.[24] The latter could count as the supplemental sentences of interpretation Lamarque mentions, though the distinction between interpretation and inductive inference seems a matter of "depth"—not, I grant, a clear demarcation. The spectator who thinks thoughts on Shakespeare's characters must, then, think (imagine, consider, hold before his mind) the propositions that Desdemona does not have Othello's handkerchief, that she is innocent of adultery, and that Othello cannot acknowledge her passionate nature—that is, he must think these to shed the "right tears" over Othello and Desdemona.

Coming to have identity between Shakespeare's propositions and our thoughts is, however, all but impossible. We come to fiction with an "intellectual and imaginative background," thoughts that may well be "far different from those directly, or logically, related to the propositional contents of the fictional sentences." One age thinks Kate of *Taming of the Shrew* a shrew to be tamed; a later age thinks of her as a proto-feminist fighting against patriarchal tyranny. Then, too, other readers may intrude, as when emoters acquire thoughts about Othello or Desdemona "in summary or paraphrase, which perhaps involves none of the descriptions written by Shakespeare." "More often than not," Lamarque writes, "we acquire the relevant thoughts [about a fictional character] from a combination of our own descriptions and a suitable subset of an author's descriptions." For these reasons, "There is no denying a genuine indeterminacy in some of our claims to be responding to *particular* fictional characters and events." As our thoughts grow more distant from the paradigm "no simple formula can settle the question whether our fear and pity are for Shakespeare's Othello and Desdemona or merely for some imaginative constructs of our own." As long as there is the "required causal history"—as long as an emoter's thoughts are traceable back to propositions about Desdemona expressed in Shakespeare's *Othello*—the

24. Stanley Cavell, *The Claim of Reason* (New York: Oxford University Press, 1979), 491.

emoter is thinking of Desdemona. But for the required causal history there is "no simple formula."[25]

With supplementary sentences we go past "strict criteria" for identity between thought and character, and this because a reader can supplement a work of fiction to his heart's content. Zany readers can construe Desdemona to be in truth as guilty as Iago makes her out to be. Such notions as "the right causal history" cannot offer a rule-governed way of constraining supplementation, for once we're beyond Shakespeare's descriptions (and perhaps their deductive consequences) we seem to be at a loss for "rightness." There is a point, though I do not know how to place it, when a reader whose thoughts depart "substantially" from Shakespeare's descriptions is no longer thinking of *Shakespeare's* Desdemona, though he may well entertain thoughts of a character he refers to as "Desdemona."

But the paradox is raised whether our tears are right or not. Suppose someone misunderstands Shakespeare—or at the least comes up with a nonstandard interpretation. Suppose he takes Desdemona to be guilty of adultery with Cassio. This somewhat colors his view of the characters, and will affect his emotions. Perhaps he will have a bit more sympathy with Othello than he would on the usual reading of the play. This reader's Desdemona is not, we'll assume, Shakespeare's Desdemona and Othello, though the reader still takes these characters to be fictions, and thus his emotions toward them are paradoxical.

There is a lacuna in Lamarque's theory, in so far as he fails to account for how thoughts of Desdemona's suffering bring on emotion given that we also believe Desdemona to be fictional. Lamarque's appeal to vividness and involvement doesn't, at least without further explanation, solve that particular difficulty. Surely we do not want to say that Shakespeare's play is so vivid and our involvement with its incidents so intense that we forget that Desdemona is only a fiction.

---

25. Lamarque, "How Can We Pity and Fear Fictions?," 301.

thought theory T

A simple counterexample to the notion that belief is
necessary for emotion is the man who feels anxious because he suspects he is late for an important
business meeting, though he doesn't believe that he is.
A viewer of *North By Northwest* also doesn't believe
that Roger Thornhill is in danger and yet that viewer
feels anxiety. But there are two important dissimilarities
between the cases. (1) The businessman presumably
believes he is on his way to a real business meeting with
real consequences if he is late; but the moviegoer
believes neither that Roger Thornhill nor his dangerous
predicament is real. The businessman's suspicion is, we
might say, existentially grounded in a way that the
moviegoer's isn't. (2) The businessman suspects that he
is late. He does not somehow at the same time believe
that he is really on time. The moviegoer, on the other
hand, believes that Roger Thornhill is in no real danger even while he experiences alarm over Thornhill's
situation. The moviegoer feels alarm not simply in the
absence of belief, but despite his disbelief.

Thought theory must show how thoughts that are not existentially grounded and that occur along with disbelief can generate emotion. Previous thought theorists have either simply finessed this problem or have pleaded agnosticism, though neither will do. What of the "causal dynamism" of thought that is not existentially grounded? Are the emotions elicited by such thought the same as those brought on in the standard way, by believing that something is really the case? In this chapter, I describe and defend a version of thought theory that I think correct, and which I'll refer to as Thought Theory T.

> *Thought Theory T.* Emotion toward what the emoter takes to be a fiction is brought on by the emoter's focused involvement with vivid and detailed thoughts that may be propositional or nonpropositional. The emoter's disbelief in any real reference of the thoughts is rendered relatively inactive. The emotion thus produced is real and typically has the character of being richly generated yet unconsummated.

The components of T are elucidated and defended below. I'll begin with the thorniest issue.

The Inactivation of Disbelief

When a person has emotions toward what he takes to be fiction, he nonetheless in some manner and at the same time believes that it is a fiction over which he emotes. This is the *diabolus* of the paradox, not to be assuaged by bewitching audiences to fictional narrative into indifference about the truth of what they entertain in thought.

Walton, of course, admits that Charles "has *no* doubts about whether he is in the presence of an actual slime."[1] Thus Charles disbelieves in the real existence of the slime (he disbelieves that he is really threatened). But what happens to Charles's disbelief? Walton's theory would appear to allow the situation described below:

A.   Charles actively believes and holds it before his mind that the slime is not at all real.

---

1. Kendall Walton, *Mimesis as Make-Believe* (Cambridge: Harvard University Press, 1990), 241.

B. Charles makes-believe that the slime is threatening.
C. Charles feels (quasi-) afraid.

However, the trio ABC is, it seems to me, psychologically impossible (or very nearly so). For disbelief, when active and present to the mind, threatens to trump—to throw cold water on—emotion. The person who concurrently and with equal mental vigor *both* entertains thoughts of the slime's threatening advance *and* brings to mind his disbelief in its real existence will, I submit, feel no fear—not even the denuded quasi-fear Walton attributes to Charles. Charles will feel nothing like an emotion, for he will be dazed by a mental traffic jam.

It may well be that Walton would agree that ABC is psychologically impossible, but would disagree that his theory allows ABC. The concept of playing games of make-believe, Walton remarks, "will enable us to account for what has been misleadingly called the suspension of disbelief without supposing that appreciators lose touch with reality when they are immersed in a work of fiction."[2] However, despite the detail that Walton bestows on his theory of make-believe, there is no further mention of how the ABC trio is going to be avoided. Is Charles so immersed in his game that he *forgets* it is just a cinematic slime? If so, why does he stay put in his seat? Or does Charles never for a moment lose sight of the fact that it is a cinematic slime that "threatens" him? If so, why does he wince, clench his chair, and let out a scream?

Previous thought theorists have not solved this problem of disbelief. Some thought theorists literally ignore it. Others, as we've seen in the previous chapter, have emoters neither believing nor disbelieving, or being indifferent to, the fictionality of the objects of their emotions. I think this latter error is a result of a faulty inference. Thought theorists hold, correctly, that if we imagine or entertain a thought p, then p is thus held in a cognitive attitude that is itself neither a form of belief nor of disbelief. Some theorists conclude that that thought is neither believed nor disbelieved. The latter inference, however, is a non sequitur. The non sequitur is enabled with terminology given currency by Roger Scruton, according to whom thoughts merely entertained are "unasserted," while thoughts believed true are "asserted." Some might conclude that one and the same thought couldn't be both asserted and unasserted at the same time. We should avoid Scruton's terminology for just this reason. In

2. Ibid.

fact we can both entertain or imagine a thought *and* disbelieve it without contradiction—though we cannot entertain or imagine a thought while *actively* disbelieving it and still manage to arouse emotion.

I want to suggest that there is a dimension of belief that I'll call its "relative activity." Though this dimension is largely ignored, it is the very crux of how thought theory can solve the paradox. Some beliefs may be highly active; others less so; still others may be entirely inactive or nearly so. I believe that the airplane I'm traveling in is about to crash; this causes all sorts of effects in me: intense anxiety, palpitations, thoughts of loved ones, and so on. This belief is highly active. On the other end of the activity spectrum, I believe that $7 + 5 = 12$. This belief causes little or no other effects in me; hence it is quite inactive. I do not mean to imply that beliefs are either active or inactive. The activity of a belief lies on a continuum ranging from beliefs I hold that have no effect on my other mental states, which would be nearly inert, to beliefs I hold that occupy my mind to the exclusion of almost everything else, beliefs that would be highly active.

I might mention that the activity or inactivity of belief does not map onto another distinction that is commonly drawn, between occurrent and nonoccurrent beliefs. Occurrent beliefs are said to be beliefs a person holds that are at the moment before his mind (he's right now, occurrently, thinking about them). Nonoccurrent beliefs are beliefs a person holds that he's not, right now, thinking about. Occurrent beliefs may be relatively inactive. I now, occurrently, believe that there is a book with a blue cover on my desk, though this barely reverberates through my other mental states and causes hardly a ripple in my daily activities—it is, in other words, a relatively inactive, occurrent belief. Nonoccurrent beliefs may be fairly active. I believe I've lost my car keys, and while I succeed in not dwelling on the matter (the belief is made to stay nonoccurrent), it colors my day for while nonoccurrent most of the time, it is highly active.

Disbelief disturbs emotion only when fairly active. Only when I actively believe that there is no Anna Karenina who suffers ostracism and loss of love will I be in danger of falling out of pity for her. It is not sufficient to keep disbelief in the factuality of fictional situations nonoccurrent (nonoccurrence is in a way irrelevant for a nonoccurrent belief may still be highly active). What matters is to give such disbelief a low level of activity. We do this both inside and outside our experience of fiction. For example, a person can postpone grief. He comes to learn of the death of a good friend, but due to present circumstances (he's at work, suppose) doesn't wish to experience grief now. He continues to believe, perhaps even occurrently, that his friend has died, though he inactivates many of the effects of this belief. Perhaps he can't inactivate *all* of its effects, but complete inactivation isn't essential. Only later, when he has some time to himself, can he let himself experience grief: feel sorrow, think on his friend's life, and regret that he will never spend time in conversation together again. The smoker who believes that his health will be irreparably harmed by smoking inactivates that belief as he lights another cigarette. He doesn't let it affect his actions (though perhaps he can't inactivate it entirely: it may produce a slight *frisson* of anxiety while he smokes). The smoker inactivates his belief about his health because he wants to enjoy his cigarette.

In saying that our belief in the unreality of a fictional character or situation should be inactive I do not mean that it should play no role whatsoever in our experience of fiction (this is the very worst understanding of the "suspension of disbelief"). I mean that our belief in the unreality of fiction should be of a *low degree* of inactivity. How low? Low enough to allow an emotional response without entrapping the spectator into believing that the fictional is real, or worse, in attempting to interact with fictions. The spectator's inactivity of disbelief should be low enough for him to pity Anna Karenina but high enough so that he doesn't attempt to communicate with her, stop her suicide, tell off her prig of a husband, and so on.

It must, in fact, be true that there is just this balance between a low level of activity of our disbelief in the reality of fictions; yet the level of activity of our disbelief must be high enough so that we do not, as we might say, lose our grip and begin to react to fictions as if they were real. The low-level activity of disbelief provides a center of gravity, so to speak, for the orbits of detached thought and the epicycles of their concomitant emotions. This psychic balance is usually maintained with respect to fictions, though now and again it is tipped. Sometimes we activate disbelief when detached thoughts threaten to bring on overly strong feelings, as when we remind ourselves during a horror film that it is only a movie. Less often, disbelief sinks into near total inactivity, and audiences shout at the movie characters or throw vegetables at the stage villain.

The question may well be raised regarding the emoter's belief that Desdemona (or whoever) is a fiction: Why is it *this* belief that is rendered relatively inactive? The answer is that beliefs in existence (or nonexistence) are easier to inactivate than other beliefs because existence, as Kant famously put it, is not a predicate—existence, that is, is not a quality of a thing. Our thoughts principally concern things and their qualities; certainly this is the case when thoughts arouse emotions. The most basic indicative sentence is subject-predicate in form, taking a thing and attributing to it some quality. When we have thoughts about a fictional object, we have thoughts principally on that object's qualities. If the fiction is a character, we think that that character is quick or dull; that he inflicts injustice or has had injustice inflicted on him; that he is suffering or causing suffering; that he is admirable, kind, brave, impetuous, or their opposites. If the fiction is a situation, we think that that situation is dangerous, or pathetic, or joyful, or annoying, and so on. We think only secondarily that it is a fiction. Existence, like assertion, is something added to the thought. Even logical notation captures this. It is one thing to simply state that a thing x has a quality F:

$$Fx$$

It is another to state that x exists

$$(\exists x)\ Fx$$

or doesn't exist

$$\neg\ (\exists x)\ Fx$$

To put it in propositionally, the sort of thought that might generate emotion (that someone is unjust or kind, for example) requires only things and their qualities (Fx), and the existential posit, $\neg\ (\exists x)\ Fx$, does not add a quality. This is why we can, apart from fiction, so easily reason using hypothetical situations, as when we test moral principles against possible cases, without becoming distracted by the fact that the cases are not actual.[3] This is also why we can easily think on Desdemona's unjust treatment at the hands of Othello without also thereby dwelling on her nonactuality.

Circumstances aid and abet the inactivation of disbelief. We learn that the appropriate appreciation of works of fiction does not include pointing out their nonactuality. We also learn that, barring exceptional circum-

---

3. Richard Moran brings out the similarities between appreciating fiction and other sorts of though experiments. For example, in moral reasoning "the response to imagined cases is part of what reveals the principled nature of a moral judgment (or its failure)." Richard Moran, "The Expression of Feeling in Imagination," *Philosophical Review* 103 (1994): 94.

stances (such as avoiding confusion), there is little benefit in keeping non-actuality active and before our minds, and more benefit to inactivating it. The benefit principally lies in the pleasure we take in narration, though it has been argued that experiencing emotion toward fiction is a way of exercising our affective responses toward reality.[4] To keep the nonactuality of fictional characters before the mind dampens our pleasure, for at least this reason. It inhibits the emotional response to fiction, which at least much of the time is itself pleasurable. As Plato well recognized, consumers of narrative fiction seek out the "baser" pleasures of emotional arousal. And a fully activated disbelief censors the emotional arousal and its concomitant pleasures. So we have hedonistic reasons for inactivating disbelief (though see the last chapter on the paradox of tragedy for complications).

The Causal Dynamism of Thought

Thought theorists would likely agree that thought is, in words of Susan Feagin, the functional equivalent of belief.[5] This implies that entertaining the thought that p or acquiring the belief that p should have equal power to inspire emotion. But this claim might require more support than is sometimes given it.

Game playing, Walton tells us, "lies at the heart of the experience of being 'caught up in a story.'"[6] Walton refers to the simple entertaining of thoughts as "a clinical intellectual exercise,"[7] with the implication that a clinical intellectual exercise could not generate emotions. Obviously thought theory disagrees, though it is incumbent on thought theory, especially on Thought Theory T, to explain how it is that the entertaining of thoughts can catch us up in the story and produce emotion.

Walton is not alone in questioning whether thought alone can generate emotion. Bijoy Boruah, in his book on the paradox, rejects Roger Scruton's view on the grounds that Scruton doesn't fully grasp the importance of

4. See Susan Feagin, "Valuing the Artworld," in Robert J. Yanal, ed., *Institutions of Art* (University Park: Pennsylvania State University Press, 1994).

5. Susan Feagin writes that "a thought can function the same way the belief ordinarily does, so that there is no different kind of psychological process involved but the same process where either thoughts or beliefs can play a certain role." Susan Feagin, *Reading With Feeling* (Ithaca: Cornell University Press, 1996), 139.

6. Walton, *Mimesis as Make-Believe*, 241.

7. Kendall Walton, "Spelunking, Simulation, and Slime," in Mette Hjort and Sue Laver, eds., *Emotion and the Arts* (New York: Oxford University Press, 1997), 38.

belief in causing emotion, and so is left (Boruah thinks) without a mental state with sufficient "causal dynamism" to bring about an emotion. While Boruah's attack is directed against Scruton's theory, it can stand as an attack on thought theory in general. Boruah's argument is approximately this: Imagination in Scruton's theory (and thought theory generally) essentially revolves around unasserted thoughts, and these are "existentially uncommitted," that is, we don't really care whether these thoughts refer. The person whose thoughts are asserted cares about what they refer to. It is this caring (Boruah calls it a "committed" frame of mind) that supplies the causal force to our emotions. Thus without commitment, we are left without any cause of emotion. Imagination, then, when lacking commitment, cannot be a source of emotion.[8]

However, there are inferences in Boruah's argument that are undefended and, I think, invalid. On the one hand it seems true to say that a person can't feel emotion for something without "caring" about it; on the other, there is no necessary connection between "caring" and existential commitment. In other words, Boruah lacks a reason why we can't care about what is merely present to the mind (in "imagination" he would say), without existential commitment.

In any event, Boruah's own solution to the paradox brings in existential belief by way of something he calls evaluative belief. The fear of the enraged lion in the painting is not "founded on the existential belief that there is an enraged lion." The viewer's imagination is further informed by his knowledge that lions are dangerous animals. This knowledge is called an "evaluative belief." Apparently this evaluative belief in the dangerousness of lions carries enough causal dynamism with it so that the viewer "does believe it to be a threat to his life."[9]

How can it be that the thought that enraged lions in general are dangerous cause us to feel fear in the presence of a painting of an enraged lion, so that our fear counts not simply as a shudder at a general danger in the world but as involving the lion in the painting? Boruah tells us that the evaluative belief "so permeates the unasserted thought . . . [that] the fictionality of what is imagined is set aside, thereby letting the subject concentrate his attention on the sense or significance of the unasserted thought."[10]

    8. Bijoy H. Boruah, *Fiction and Emotion: A Study in Aesthetics and the Philosophy of Mind* (Oxford: Clarendon Press, 1988), 92–93.
    9. Ibid., 100.
    10. Ibid., 103.

Can this really be correct? The viewer of the painting of the enraged lion begins, Boruah seems to suggest, with an unasserted thought about an enraged lion, though with no existential beliefs in the lion. His mental state thus consists of at least these states.

Viewer imagines: he is before an enraged lion. &

Viewer believes: $\neg\ (\exists x)\ (x =$ an enraged lion before him)

But during his contemplation of the painting it occurs to him that he also believes that enraged lions are dangerous:

Viewer believes: enraged lions are dangerous

This latter "evaluative" belief so "permeates" his imagination that the viewer "sets aside the fictionality of what is imagined." What else could "setting aside the fictionality of what is imagined" come to if not:

Viewer no longer believes: $\neg\ (\exists x)\ (x =$ an enraged lion before him)

But then won't it be the case that:

Viewer imagines: he is before an enraged lion. &

Viewer believes: $(\exists x)\ (x =$ an enraged lion)

Now our viewer certainly has sufficient causal dynamism for being afraid, but at the cost of losing his grasp on reality! Whatever else is true of the matter, viewers of paintings of enraged lions do not respond as fearfully as they would in the presence of enraged lions.

Hopefully, therefore, there is something other than existential commitment to provide the energy that makes thought produce emotion. The power of thought, perhaps, lies with the sort of thoughts one thinks (their vividness and detail, for example), as well as how much the thinker is involved with them. These are suggestions outlined by Peter Lamarque, though I would like to expand and defend them.

Involvement with a thought is in Lamarque's essay the "level of attention we give to it, which can be increased . . . by bringing to mind accompanying mental images or by 'following through' its consequences. For this reason it is often not so much single thoughts that are frightening . . . as thought-clusters.[11] For example, were I holed up in a cabin below a snowy mountain and think, simply, of an avalanche, I might not feel horror, or might feel only a tiny bit of horror. But when I manufacture a vivid scenario of the avalanche—its roar, its rushing snow, me buried alive—I will feel horror in abundance. While this seems true, it really runs involvement into vividness and detail.

To speak of involvement with thought by itself we have to think in terms of attention and distraction. A thinker is involved with his thoughts to the extent that he entertains it without distractions, either external or internal. The playgoer who is distracted by talking in the row behind him has a low degree of involvement with his thought, and will predictably show little emotion toward the fictions depicted. And in Bullough's famous example, the husband distracted by worries about his wife's fidelity will not respond emotionally to Othello's brutality. To bring on emotion we need a focused involvement with out thoughts, which is an attention span unbroken by any competing thoughts that don't contribute to the emotion-generating thought cluster. It isn't that we can't think of diverse things more or less at the same time; but I don't think such thought processes have much emotional power.

Lamarque mentions vividness, and while I think vividness important for generating emotion, we have to try to understand what it is. At least one recent writer has warned us not to understand vividness as naturalness: the more vivid work is not necessarily the work that is more true-to-life. Richard Moran writes, "Going from a straight, 'flat,' uninspiring description of some event to an emotionally charged one is typically *not* a matter of making the account more and more faithful to real life." Moran claims that what engages the audience's emotion in Macbeth's soliloquy on sleep is not its true-to-lifeness but its expressive qualities:

> — the innocent sleep,
> Sleep that knits up the ravelled sleave of care,
> The death of each day's life, sore labor's bath,
> Balm of hurt minds, great nature's second course,
> Chief nourisher in life's feast. (Act 2, scene 2)

"The language put into the mouth of someone like Macbeth is fairly remote from anything one could imagine anyone really speaking." Our

---

11. Peter Lamarque, "How Can We Fear and Pity Fictions?," *British Journal of Aesthetics* 21 (1981): 295.

emotions would not be raised more strongly "if, instead of this speech, Macbeth had simply said, 'I could really use a rest.'" What arouses emotion are "the expressive qualities of a work," such as "the resources of figuration, allusion, rhythm, repetition, assonance, and dissonance; all elements that make what we are reading or hearing less like something that we could make-believe is real, or a true record of anything." It is such expressive qualities "that typically make the difference between representations that are arousing and those that aren't . . . but typically contribute nothing of their own to the generation of fictional truths about the world depicted."[12]

Moran's position, however, is ambiguous between (a) only expressive qualities (quite apart from anything representational) arouse emotion; and (b) representation requires expressive qualities to arouse emotion (i.e., "bare" or "flat" representation is unarousing). If he intends (a), he must regard something that is purely expressive—a painting by Rothko or a passage from Gertrude Stein or James Joyce—as emotionally arousing, perhaps even more arousing that passages "cluttered up" with representational detail. Poe's poem, "The Bells," for example, is chock-a-block with "figuration, allusion, rhythm, repetition, assonance, and dissonance":

> Hear the sledges with the bells—
> Silver bells!
> What a world of merriment their melody foretells!
> How they tinkle, tinkle, tinkle,
> In the icy air of night!
> While the stars that oversprinkle
> All the heaven seem to twinkle
> With a crystalline delight;
> Keeping time, time, time,
> in a sort of Runic rhyme,
> To the tintinnabulation that so musically wells
> From the bells, bells, bells, bells,
> Bells, bells, bells—
> From the jingling and the tinkling of the bells.

But I'm not sure that Poe's poem arouses emotion (complete with intentional object), though the silver bell stanza does call up a lighthearted mood. But even if some find the poem emotionally arousing (are brought to feel merry because these relentless bells are tinkling, for example), it is unconvincing to say that Poe's verse is more arousing than Tolstoy's descriptions of Anna Karenina's plight, descriptions which have considerably less in the way of rhyme, rhythm, and the other qualities Moran mentions.

This leaves Moran with claim (b), namely, that "flat" descriptions—descriptions bereft of expressive qualities—are not emotionally arousing. With this we might well agree, though it seems a circular claim: only emotionally charged descriptions are emotionally arousing. The interesting question is to try to put our fingers on what is emotionally arousing about narrative. The qualities Moran mentions (rhyme, repetition, and the rest) must be counted as some expressive qualities that *sometimes* work to arouse emotion (and sometimes not: not every rhymed repetition works). But they can't be a complete catalog.

I propose to understand "vividness" not as "naturalism" but as "barrage of details." Aristotle placed so much reliance on plot that he was moved to write, "The story should be so constructed that the events make anyone who hears the story shudder and feel pity even without seeing the play."[13] Perhaps this is so for certain plot structures, though this strikes me as one time Aristotle is wrong (if he means that we will be moved to pity *just as if* we had seen the play). Moran points out that we are not as moved by a Cliff's Notes summary of *Macbeth* as we are by the play itself, from which he concludes that it must be the expressive qualities of Shakespeare's poetry that are emotionally arousing. But it is not only these poetic devices that plot summaries leave behind. What plot summaries also lack are details, for it is the particular ways the plot is worked—its details—which pack much of the emotional punch.

Let's contrast two works of fiction. The first is Anne Rice's now famous story of the vampire Lestat and his "fledgling" vampire Louis who at this point in the story are in a bordello in eighteenth-century New Orleans with two women. The second is my "remake" of it. Lestat has already drunk the blood of one of the women, and now turns his attentions to the other:

> "[Lestat] took the girl's wrist again, and she cried out as the knife cut. She opened her eyes slowly as he held her wrist over the glass. She blinked and

13. Aristotle, *The Poetics*, XIV, from G. M. A. Grube, trans., *Aristotle on Poetry and Style* (New York: Macmillan Publishing, 1958), 26–27.

strained to keep them open. It was as if a veil covered her eyes. 'You're tired, aren't you?' he asked her. She gazed at him as if she couldn't really see him. 'Tired!' he said, now leaning close and staring into her yes. 'You want to sleep.' 'Yes . . .' she moaned softly. And he picked her up and took her into the bedroom. Our coffins rested on the carpet and against the wall; there was a velvet-draped bed. Lestat did not put her on the bed; he lowered her slowly into his coffin. 'What are you doing?' I asked him, coming to the door sill. The girl was looking around like a terrified child. 'No . . .' she was moaning. And then, as he closed the lid, she screamed. She continued to scream within the coffin" (Anne Rice, *Interview with the Vampire*)

Lestat cut the girl's wrist with a knife and emptied her blood into a glass. She seemed tired. Eventually Lestat picked her up, carried her to the bedroom, whereupon he lowered her into his coffin. The girl seemed quite terrified by all this.

The first passage will inspire horror in most readers. The second will not. Why does it work the way Anne Rice wrote it but not the way Robert Yanal did? The key here is detail. Rice's details engage the reader's imagination—to interest him, perhaps help him envision it—in a way that Yanal does not. Details allow the reader more grist for his emotional mill. It isn't merely that a young girl is bled for the pleasure of the vampire Lestat; she is drained slowly, she is near to the point of unconsciousness though conscious enough to realize the horror of her own situation; she asks to be put to bed but is taken instead to a coffin in which she is locked away, alive and awake.

And it isn't only *particular* details—the girl being locked, alive, in a coffin—that occasion emotion. It is also the *barrage* of detail. Length in narrative serves a function beyond giving readers a good, long read or moviegoers two hours of story for their admission fee. The sheer build-up of detail narrative length provides a cumulative emotional effect of its own. It is not simply a *façon de parler* to say that our horror mounts as we read Anne Rice. Emotion is made the more palpable the longer it is maintained; and the more details (of horror, of suffering, of heroism) the longer an emotion (fear, pity, admiration) is maintained.

But, of course, detail is not itself sufficient. Remakes are sometimes less emotionally arousing than their originals, but not for lack of detail. A work counts as a remake of another, earlier work if it preserves the essentials of the earlier work's plot. Henri-George Cluzot's 1955 film

Diabolique makes us feel "queasy and sordid and scared" (Pauline Kael); but its 1996 version, which follows the original almost scene for scene, left me unmoved. Emil Jannings's fate at the end of Von Sternberg's *The Blue Angel* was deeply moving, but Theodore Bickel's fate in the same role in the 1959 remake was not. The difference between the emotionally arousing original and the emotionally inert remake is not the difference between abundance and dearth of detail, but between the right and the wrong details. Here we must make some appeal to the expressive power of Cluzot's or Sternberg's movie making, though obviously these will not be captured in Moran's list of figuration, allusion, and so on.

Focused involvement with thoughts is, according to thought theory T, required for emotional arousal. In this we have an answer to why certain narratives fail to be emotionally arousing. Famously, the death of Little Nell in *The Old Curiosity Shop* brought laughter not tears to Oscar Wilde. And Noël Carroll reminds us of some of the worst films ever made:

> *Plan 9 from Outer Space*, a feature film shamelessly patched together around some footage of Bela Lugosi before he died, strikes many as ridiculous rather than horrifying. But, even more importantly, there are many horror films which fail to horrify, not because they are ridiculous, but because they are altogether lackluster. Perhaps *The Brain from Planet Arous* is an example here. Moreover, with respect to other genres, there are many melodramas that we find emotionally inert and adventures that are not suspenseful.[14]

The problem with *Plan 9* is that it isn't at all horrifying though it was intended to be. Its plot structure, though, is not entirely unpromising: space aliens believe they can conquer Earth by resurrecting corpses from a San Fernando Valley cemetery. It is *conceivable* that someone might make quite a horrifying film from this plot line. Ed Wood Jr., the director of *Plan 9* (and himself the subject of a film biography by Tim Burton) did not. Such works are like a joke that isn't funny: we know it is intended to be funny, for we discern a structure of a joke, but it doesn't produce

14. Noël Carroll, "On Kendall Walton's *Mimesis as Make-Believe*," *Philosophy and Phenomenological Research* 51 (1991): 385. Carroll is objecting that Walton's theory of make-believe can't explain why some "props" (i.e., works of fiction) in games of make-believe inspire emotions while some do not.

laughter or amusement. In *Plan 9*, we discern the structure of danger (aliens, graveyards, a corpse revived by electrode rays) and hence the intent to arouse fear. Indeed, Carroll uses the example as a puzzle for Walton's theory. We can make-believe (using *Plan 9* as a prop) that aliens have invaded earth, that they have resurrected corpses, and so on, and as far as Walton's theory goes, we should be horrified, yet we're not. Walton is unable to account for the quality of props since his theory has us entertaining certain fictional truths, that is, propositions that are authorized for pretense by the work at issue; and the quality of a work is not one of its fictional truths.

Why does *Plan 9* fail? One simple answer is that the thoughts it inspires are not horrifying, but this itself needs explanation. One might say that the horror touches are missing, but this is on its face not exactly true: *Plan 9* has enlivened corpses, graveyards, and space aliens. Perhaps the answer lies in distracting thoughts. Emotion may need a *sustained* thought-sequence of emotion-inducing aspects, and failed art delivers a scatter, interrupted and hence thwarted by bad acting, bad writing, silly costumes, and other fatal flaws. After all, whom will a film frighten while distracted by such lines as, "Remember my friends, future events such as these will affect you in the future"? (Perhaps we also require our horror genres to be pure, and balk at admixtures of space aliens with zombies.)

Thought theory need not be limited to thoughts on the representational or narrative features alone. Contrast two performances of *Othello*. In one, the actress portraying Desdemona is doing a superb job of acting; in the other, the actress is quite bad. A theory such as Walton's effectively insulates the emoter from what we might call the mode of presentation of the fictional truths. On Walton's theory, it apparently does not matter whether the actress portraying Desdemona gives a good or a bad performance, as long as the same fictional truths are generated. The emoter can still make-believe that badly-acted or well-acted Desdemona is about to be strangled by Othello, and for all Walton says the emoter will feel horrified in either case. But this can't be right. We will likely not care about the fate of badly acted Desdemona (or we might perversely feel *glad* that she's about to be strangled). Thought theory can allow artlessness to influence thought, and this seems to be why bad art fails to inspire emotion: the annoying ineptitudes of it overwhelm and cancel out what emotion-inducing aspects it has.

Nonpropositional Thoughts

Philosophical theories of emotion and fiction tend to speak in terms of propositions. Walton's theory of emotion toward fiction, for example, has prospective emoters making believe that certain propositions are fictionally true. Peter Lamarque, whom I take to be the one of the best exemplars of thought theory in the extant literature, also tends to proceed propositionally. The prospective emoter, before he can pity Desdemona, should establish "identity of content" between his thoughts and propositions about her expressed in Shakespeare's play and propositions derived in appropriate ways from those. Fictional characters for Lamarque are the senses of their names, and to think about a fictional character is to reproduce such senses in thought.[15] Now it is true that Lamarque allows there to be such a thing as "predicative thought," which is not exactly propositional, but his theory *on the whole* proceeds propositionally.

But can propositional thought account for all emotional arousal toward fiction? Richard Moran points out that the viewer who "reduces" Van Gogh's *Starry Night* to the simply fictional truth that there are stars in a night sky will miss the emotional involvement with Van Gogh's brush strokes. In Moran's view, "The very expressive qualities that disrupt any sense of a fictional world are in fact central for our psychological participation with artworks."[16] I would put it somewhat differently: There are qualities of narrative fiction that are not captured in propositions but when captured in thought brings on emotion.

Consider the famous montage sequence in *High Noon* during which the clock ticks the final minutes toward the arrival of the noon train carrying the just released convict Frank Miller (Ian MacDonald) who has threatened vengeance against Will Kane (Gary Cooper), the Marshall who put him in prison. Prior to this sequence, Cooper's deputy deserts him, and none of the men at the local saloon will serve as deputies. At a local church where Cooper goes for help, the parishioners argue against putting up a fight; and the town leader Jonas Henderson (Thomas Mitchell) says that it's a personal matter between Cooper and MacDonald, best settled between them. Cooper is left to face the killers alone.

---

15. See Peter Lamarque, "Fictional Characters," in his book of essays, *Fictional Points of View* (Ithaca: Cornell University Press, 1996), 33ff.
16. Moran, "Expression of Feeling," 83.

The montage shows Marshall Kane seated at his desk; a clock showing a minute before noon; McDonald's brother and two gunslingers waiting at the train depot and looking down the empty tracks; the church filled with cowed, frightened people; the town's streets empty; and finally we hear the train whistle. The montage is wordless, the only sound being the ticking of the clock against Dmitri Tiomkin's score hammered out louder and louder—and finally the train whistles. During the sequence, the audience's concern for Marshall Kane mounts to a high pitch. The montage is nonsentential, nonlinguistic. We grasp it that way. That is, we do not mentally "translate" the images of the montage into the proposition that the McDonalds are waiting for the train in order to stimulate emotion. So it is the sounds and images of the montage that are entertained in thought and nonpropositionally arouse our anxiety.

It isn't only cinematic montage that seems nonpropositional. Max Schreck's look in Murnau's 1922 *Nosferatu is* to me horrifingly loathsome (quite in contrast to later aristocratic and handsome vampires— Christopher Lee, Louis Jordan, Frank Langella, Tom Cruise), though I have been at screenings where his first appearance has elicited giggles (well, there are those *ears*). The preternatural "breathing" of the house in *The Haunting*, the blood-curdling howls in *The Hound of the Baskervilles*, Robert Mitchum's hymn ("Leaning, leaning! Safe and secure from all alarms. Leaning, leaning. Leaning on the everlasting arms!") that foretokens his presence to the fleeing children in *Night of the Hunter*—all these contribute to the fear felt by viewers of these movies, though the first two are not propositional at all, and the third arouses anxiety in contrast to its message of safety and security.

The sheer chill of the hound's howls or the loathsome look of Max Schreck's vampire cannot be captured in such a "fictional truth" as *There is a dog howling hideously* or *There is a loathsome-appearing man standing outside*, and hence the fear or disgust that is generated must be generated by thinking something other than propositions. Lamarque may try to subsume this as a "predicative description," though to me this is both too close to propositions, suggesting Frege's "unsaturated thoughts" (_____ *is red*), as well as sounding inaccurate. Who would call a hound's howl or a vampire's look a predicate? It is far simpler to recognize these as giving rise to nonpropositional thoughts. What Thought Theory T counts as emotionally arousing is not entertaining in thought simply propositions but the panoply of narrative resources, both propositional and nonpropositional.

An Objection to Thought Theory

Thought theorists sometimes get themselves into trouble. Peter Lamarque, for example, writes, "the real objects of our fear in fictional cases are thoughts."[17] Such remarks lead Walton to object:

> What we call "fear of the slime" by ordinary appreciators fully aware of its fictitiousness is in general, [Lamarque] thinks, fear of the thought. I see no advantage in this suggestion. The reasons for denying that Charles fears the slime apply equally to the thought. Apart from special circumstances, as when he has a heart condition, he does not consider the thought dangerous or treat it as such, nor does he experience even an inclination to escape from it. Moreover, his experience simply does not feel like fear of a thought; characterizing it as such flies in the face of its phenomenology. And it is the *slime*, not a thought, that Charles so inevitably and unabashedly describes himself as afraid of.[18]

Yet it could be said with equal plausibility that Charles is on Walton's theory frightened by a make-believe truth, and that this flies in the face of the phenomenology of emotion toward fiction, for it is the slime and not a make-believe truth that Charles describes himself as afraid of. The fact is that on either make-believe or thought theory Charles is frightened by some internal (mental) representation. He is frightened by the intentional object of his mental processes, by the *content* of what he thinks.

When I pity Desdemona, what do I pity? It seems true both that there is nothing I pity (for there is no Desdemona) *and* that there is something I pity (for I will say that I pity Desdemona). Contradictory answers often point to an ambiguous question, and the question, What do I pity when I pity Desdemona?, is indeed ambiguous. It asks simultaneously for the direct (or real) object of my pity, and for the intentional (or mental) object of my pity. The direct object of my pity is nothing at all (or, allowing for philosophical reifications of fictional objects, nothing material and particular); for Desdemona is a fiction. The intentional object of my pity is a thought (or mental representation) of a certain sort—Desdemona as falsely and cruelly accused of infidelity by her husband.

Edward Gron claims of our pity for Willy Loman (of Arthur Miller's *Death of a Salesman*), "it is only the idea of Loman that fills [us] with pity.

17. Lamarque, "How Can We Fear and Pity Fictions?," 294.
18. Walton, *Mimesis as Make-Believe*, 203.

And this pity is such that nothing is the object of it." On Gron's view, our pity "is a kind of free-floating pity" which has no object, though, "like Russell's proper names, 'always wishes to have' an object."[19] Gron wishes to meet Walton's objection that it is a thought (or idea) that we pity in pitying Willy Loman. But he does so at the cost of asserting that our pity has no object at all: no direct (or real) object, and no intentional (or mental) object. Now it's of course true that our pity for Willy Loman has no real object; this follows from Loman's fictionality. But is it true that our pity has no intentional or mental object, and is thus free-floating?

If the intended question is What is the direct (real) object of my pity?, then the answer ought not to be: a thought or mental representation. By the same token, if the intended question is What is the intentional (mental) object of my pity?, then the answer ought not to be: nothing at all. Elizabeth Anscombe reminded us of this in a classic paper (from which I borrow the terminology of "intentional" versus "direct" object).[20] It is a truth, Anscombe says, that the Greeks worshipped Zeus, yet it is also true that there is no Zeus. (These can both be true together because "X worships _____" is an intentional context.) What, then, did the Greeks worship? Anscombe points out that it is "a not very happy move" to understand "Zeus" to be "an idea," at least if we take this to imply that the Greeks worshipped an idea. For that is not what the Greeks took themselves to be worshipping. The unhappiness comes from shifting the question, What did the Greeks worship?, from a request for the intentional object of worship to a query about the direct object of worship. The intentional object of the Greeks' worship was an idea (or mental representation); at the same time, there was no real object of their worship. An intentional object for Anscombe "is given by a word or phrase which gives a *description under which*" the worshipper would recognize Zeus. And Zeus—the intentional object of his worshippers—is not given by the description "an idea." But it is given by such a phrase as "ruler of all men and gods," and the Greeks would probably have agreed that in worshipping Zeus they worshipped the ruler of all men and gods.

In the same way, the emoter who pities Desdemona, who does not exist, does not pity an object described as "a thought" (for no emoter would take himself to pity a thought) but rather an object described as

19. Edward Gron, "Defending Thought Theory From a Make-Believe Threat," *British Journal of Aesthetics* 36 (1996): 311–12.

20. G. E. M. Anscombe, "The Intentionality of Sensations," in R. J. Butler, ed., *Analytical Philosophy: Second Series* (New York: Barnes & Noble, Inc., 1965).

"the innocent victim of Othello's jealousy" or other appropriate phrases. Such descriptions are of the content of the thought (or perhaps its sense), and of course it is the contents of thoughts properly speaking that inspire emotion.

Emotions Richly Generated Yet Unconsummated

Is there a *thoroughgoing* difference between emotion toward what is taken to be fiction and emotion toward what is taken to be fact? Kendall Walton thinks that such emotions are mere quasi-emotions, by which he means mental states that have the phenomenological features of emotions (the palpitations of fear, for example) but are generated by make-believe and unconsummated in action. Peter Lamarque, on the other hand, straightforwardly writes, "The fear associated with a frightening thought is a genuine, not a 'quasi' or fictional fear."[21] I think Lamarque roughly correct.

In Chapter 4, I argued that inaction is not a characteristic *unique* to emotion toward fiction, that there are perfectly ordinary instances of emotion toward what we take to be fact that do not eventuate in action. Yet what shall we say about Charles who screams but does not flee? Or about the reader who disapproves of Humbert's marriage to Lolita's mother in order to be near her daughter, and who neither admonishes Humbert nor alerts the mother? It would seem that inactivity, while perhaps not unique to emotion toward fiction, is its near-constant companion. This appearance, though, is not quite the full story.

I think emoters sometimes *wish* they could act, or better, interact with characters they take to be fictions. Call this wish irrational if you like, though it seems no more irrational than other wishes you entertain that you know can't be satisfied: to take back the hurtful remark you just made, for example, or to see through a fog. Such wishes seem to provoke a sort of impulse to action that is thwarted by the acknowledgment that the act can't be done, can't possibly bring off its intended goal. But the impulse is there, though it does not produce movement, as Aristotle would put it.

I want to review the parallel universe case of Chapter 4. In that case we suppose there to be a universe parallel to ours, separated from us by one-

---

21. Lamarque, "How Can We Pity and Fear Fictions?," 295.

way Plexiglas. We can see into that universe, though its inhabitants cannot see into ours. Its inhabitants never suspect that they live next to (if that is the term) our universe. Hence its inhabitants never suspect our existence. Further, the laws of physics make it such that the mirror is impenetrable except by photons, and these only one way. We have no hope of ever entering or communicating this parallel universe. In the parallel universe, we see people much like ourselves. That is, we have every reason to think that these inhabitants are real people, and not moving pictures or animated robots—at least they seem as real as the people we see outside our windows every day.

We see the inhabitants of the parallel universe fall in and out of love, do great good and great evil, lose spouses and lovers to death, and become the victims of cruelty and injustice. As we watch we have emotions for them: we sympathize with this one's loss, we disapprove of that one's actions, we feel elated that the other won the contest, and so on. Now we can't, physically, interact or communicate with them, though we sometimes wish we could. Our emotions are thus thwarted in movement by our knowledge that action cannot succeed, though our emotions might not necessarily be lacking in impulse or motive. We wish we could congratulate the young woman on winning the race, though we know we can't.

The parallel universe is, I submit, a fair (thought not exact) analogue to our situation with respect to fictions. We look in at the fictions, though they can't look out at us. We know we cannot, metaphysically, interact with fictions (for they don't exist). But we sometimes wish we could. I think we—some of us, sometimes—wish that we could console Lear as he cradles the dead Cordelia, and this comes close to a motive to act. We might wish to though we can't, ever, ask Othello why he trusts Iago so completely. We might want to, though we are forever barred from dancing with the characters played by Fred Astaire or Ginger Rogers. We fear for private detective Milton Arbogast (Martin Balsam) as he makes his way up the stairs in the old Bates mansion, and though we might want to, we cannot warn him. We pity Anna Karenina, though we can neither commiserate with her nor suggest that she is complaining too much. Our emotions in all these cases remain unconsummated. Even if they begin to enter into something like a wish to act, they never do reach that goal.

Theory T suggests that the emotions we experience toward fiction typically exhibit this *unconsummated* quality. An emotion is consummated (as I'll use the term) when we undertake an action toward a goal posed in part by the emotion, and in addition, we bring this goal about. Otherwise, the emotion is unconsummated. We fear an avalanche, so we evacuate our camp near the base of the mountain. Our fear enters into our action—evacuating our camp—as posing a goal: we want to get away from the avalanche because, in part, we fear it. When we evacuate the camp, our fear is consummated. When we don't act on any motives that might come from out pity for old King Lear, our pity is unconsummated.

When we read or view works of fiction, we are usually fed prodigious amounts of information. (The novels of Samuel Beckett may be an exception, but their sparseness brings out the richness of what they are exception to.) We become privy to characters' thoughts, to intimate scenes, to what's going on both here and back at the ranch. Such prodigious amounts of information, when they inspire thoughts that are entertained and, in the fullness of time, give rise to emotion, means that such emotions are *richly generated*. We can better see this with a thought-experiment.

Suppose the actual world was to present us with a real Anna Karenina: the novel is, to the extent possible, made real (I don't mean enacted; I mean encountered in reality). The world contains, not only Tolstoy's novel but also a real-Anna who actual life matches fictional-Anna's. We'll also have to suppose that Tolstoy did not write about real-Anna; real-Anna comes about after Tolstoy's novel is published. Suppose also that no miracles occur. By no miracles occurring I mean that we are subject to the laws of nature and not poetic license. We are not granted access to real-Anna's unspoken thoughts, we cannot be in two places at once, and so on. We become witnesses to real-Anna's decline and fall to the extent normal interaction in the real world permits. As witnesses to real-Anna, we would, approximately, know the sort of information about her that her close friends have.

But as readers of Tolstoy's novel, we have far and away more information. We often know fictional-Anna's thoughts, but of course we only sometimes know real-Anna's thoughts (and then, only when she expresses them—but how will we be sure she is expressing herself honestly?). We would be witnesses to intimate scenes between fictional-Anna and her husband and between her and Vronsky; yet real-Anna would not allow even her best friends to be present at such occasions. We would be both at fictional-Levin's country estate and in St. Petersburg simultaneously; but we couldn't do this in the real world. In addition, some readers read and re-read *Anna Karenina*. They therefore become *very* familiar with fictional-Anna's story. As real-life witnesses to real-Anna, we will lose many of the details of her decline and fall: we now and again mishear what real-

Anna said; we see real-Anna do something or bear a certain countenance but later forget; there's sometimes just too much going on to notice it all; and so on—like life itself. Suppose we pity both fictional-Anna and real-Anna. Our pity toward real-Anna will be more richly generated (it derives from more information) than our pity toward fictional-Anna.

Emotions that are richly generated yet remain unconsummated, typical of emotions toward fiction, occur though infrequently outside fiction. We rarely get so much information about someone with so little interaction with him or her. Tchaikovsky's relation with Nadezhda van Meck comes to mind as a singular exception. The wealthy Mme. van Meck became Tchaikovsky's patron and provided him with an annuity. Oddly, she stipulated that they never meet, a condition that was apparently honored, though he was to dedicate his Fourth Symphony to her. After a correspondence of some fourteen years, Mme. van Meck terminated her epistolary relationship and financial support abruptly and without explanation. Whatever might have been Tchaikovsky's emotions toward Nadezhda van Meck, they were probably something like our emotions toward fictions: emotions based on much information though unconsummated.

"What is pity or anger which is never to be acted on? What is love that cannot be expressed to its object and is logically or metaphysically incapable of consummation?," Walton asks.[22] He thinks such pity, anger, or love mere quasi-emotions, less than real. But I think what we have is real pity that must be kept to oneself, real anger that is forever ineffectual, real love that is never to be returned.

---

22. Walton, *Mimesis as Make-Believe*, 196.

the paradox
of suspense

Suspense, Repetition, and Paradox

There are other paradoxes percolating up from our experience of fiction, other than the Big One of accounting for emotions toward what we know to be fictional. One of these is the paradox of suspense. Suspense appears different from other emotions we may have toward fiction. We may, over and over, hate Iago because he has driven Othello to murder his beloved Desdemona, but we can't, over and over, be in suspense over what Othello does—unless we're, over and over, uncertain about what Othello does. And yet people who have seen or read *Othello*, and certainly those who remember what happens, are people who are not uncertain as to whether Othello does or does not do something dire to Desdemona. The paradox arises if such people, whom I'll call "repeaters," feel suspense upon re-viewing *Othello* though they know its awful ending. The paradox can be described as an inconsistency among this trio of apparent truths:

(S1) Suspense is an emotion generated only in the presence of uncertainty of the outcome of a certain narrative situation.

(S2) Some people ("repeaters") experience suspense though they know the outcome of that narrative situation from previous encounters (they've read the story before, have already seen the movie, etc.).

(S3) For the repeater, there is no uncertainty regarding the outcome of that situation.

In Alfred Hitchcock's wartime film *Notorious* (1944), Alicia Huberman (Ingrid Bergman), daughter of a man convicted of spying for the Nazis, is herself recruited to spy for the American government when it is discovered that she doesn't share her father's politics. Alicia has (as part of her "secret mission") married Alexander Sebastian (Claude Rains), a former friend of her father's, who runs a chemical plant and a ring of Nazi spies in Rio de Janeiro. Suspicion begins to center on Sebastian's wine cellar which is thought to harbor something other than wine, something very important to the Nazi cause (it turns out to be uranium).[1] Now the American spy Devlin (Cary Grant) must gain access to the wine cellar. But how will Alicia engineer this without arousing suspicion? She invites Devlin to a large reception given by herself and her husband. In one sweeping take, the camera begins at the top of a stairway overlooking a crowd of Nazi party guests, moves down the stairs, through the assembled guests, and into the main ballroom, where it zeros in on Sebastian's key ring. Alicia removes a key, secretes it in her palm, and the camera follows her as she greets invited guest Devlin with a handshake.

The two eventually make their way into the wine cellar where they discover a dark metallic ore stored in wine bottles, while above them the reception of Nazi agents goes on. It is entirely clear that their lives are in danger if they are discovered, and they almost are. Sebastian comes down the stairs, too late for them to hide; so Devlin grabs Alicia and kisses her thus masking a spy mission as a pass at the host's wife, a ruse which Sebastian seems to accept (though he will later develop his own suspicions about Alicia).

First-time viewers of *Notorious* don't know whether Alicia and Devlin will be found out in the wine cellar; and because of their uncertainty, first-

---

1. The idea of uranium was fairly prescient on Hitchcock's part—remember that *Notorious* was shot before the bomb was dropped on Hiroshima.

time viewers experience intense suspense as Alicia and Devlin rummage through the wine bottles. Will Alicia be missed upstairs? Will anyone come down to the wine cellar? Could the spies possibly escape detection as Sebastian descends into the cellar? Suspense dissipates when Alicia and Devlin get away with this particular escapade, though Hitchcock's film begins almost immediately to rebuild suspense by introducing other dangers for Alicia.

Repeaters (those who have seen the film at least once and are into their second or third or . . . viewing) know in advance that Alicia and Devlin are not found out in the wine cellar, or so many assume. We would predict that repeaters won't experience suspense during the wine cellar scene, for they are certain as to its outcome. Yet *if* repeaters *still* experience suspense during the wine cellar sequence, we encounter paradox.

Do repeaters re-experience suspense? Kendall Walton, among others, thinks that they do. Indeed he thinks repeaters experience suspense over and over again with each retelling of the same narrative. "Will Jack of 'Jack and the Beanstalk' succeed in ripping off the Giant without being caught?," Walton asks.

> Although Lauren knows that fictionally Jack will escape from the Giant, as she listens to still another rereading of "Jack and the Beanstalk," it is fictional that she does not know this—until the reading of the passage describing his escape. Fictionally she is genuinely worried about his fate and attentively follows the events as they unfold. It is fictional in her game during a given reading or telling of the story that she learns for the first time about Jack and the Giant. . . . It is the fact that fictionally she is uncertain about the outcome, not actual uncertainty, which is responsible for the excitement and suspense of her experience. . . . One cannot learn, each time one hears the story, what fictionally Jack and the Giant do, unless one always forgets in between. But one can participate each time in a game, and that is what appreciators do.[2]

Another writer on the topic, Richard Gerrig, describes what is supposed to be a typical reader's response to Richard Rhodes's history, *The Making of the Atomic Bomb*. The reader, if he is typical, knows that the atomic bomb will eventually be made, though Rhodes's book "so painstakingly

---

2. Kendall Walton, *Mimesis as Make-Believe* (Cambridge: Harvard University Press, 1990), 261.

lays out obstacles to the development of the bomb that the book is inces-
santly suspenseful."[3] And Noël Carroll has claimed, "I myself have seen
King Kong at least 50 times, and yet there are still certain moments when I
feel the irresistible tug of suspense."[4]

The Nature of Suspense

The emotion tagged with the singleton name of "suspense" is actually a
complex of mental states and affects: a heightened sense of anticipation, a
need to know what comes next, often the fear that the "wrong" thing will
happen, and all this sometimes accompanied by increased heart rate and
bated breath. Such sensations are a sort of "rush" to many audiences who
thrive largely if not entirely on suspense stories.

When we think of tales of suspense, we think primarily of mysteries
and tales involving great danger. But all sorts of narratives, both fictional
and factual, commonly raise suspense in their audience. A narrative lays
out over time (not all at once) a sequence of events; and because the
events of the narrative are not completely told all at once, questions arise
for the audience that will be answered only later in the narrative's telling.
Will the transfigured panther-woman (Simone Simon) pounce on her
rival (Jane Randolph) as she walks home alone at night, hearing strange
noises around her? (Val Lewton's *Cat People*, 1942). Will Sam and Annie
(Tom Hanks and Meg Ryan) ever make their date at the top of the Empire
State Building? (Nora Ephron's *Sleepless in Seattle*, 1993). And the most
classic question of all: Who dunnit? Suspense is all but built-in to the
nature of narrative, except when the author tips his hand early on. "This
is the story of a murder. It hasn't happened yet. But it will," Martin Amis
writes at the beginning of *London Fields*. "I know the murderer, I know
the murderee," and we're soon told that the murderee is to be Nicola
Six.[5] But we don't know until the end who will kill her. And why.

Under what conditions will suspense be aroused? First, uncertainty
must be introduced via a narrative situation for which several outcomes

3. Richard J. Gerrig, *Experiencing Narrative Worlds: On the Psychological Activities of Reading*
(New Haven: Yale University Press, 1993), 159.
4. Noël Carroll, "The Paradox of Suspense," in P. Vorderer, H. Wulff, and M. Friedrichsen, eds.,
Suspense: Conceptualizations, Theoretical Analyses, and Empirical Explorations (Mahwah, N.J.:
Lawrence Earlbaum Associates, 1996), 71.
5. Martin Amis, *London Fields* (New York: Vintage Books, 1991).

or resolutions are implied as possible within the confines of the story. Someone on the train committed the murder, though this could be one of several characters. The hero dangles from a cliff so precariously that he might well fall before he is rescued, and his rescue seems all but impossible. The timer on the bomb is ticking away, but can it be disarmed before it explodes? The police aren't even sure where it is. Miss Bennett may or may not marry Mr. Darcy. And so on.

Second, an audience to such a narrative must want to know the outcome. A proposal from Noël Carroll suggests that suspense is raised only if "the possible outcomes of the situation set down by the story are such that the outcome that is morally correct, in terms of the values inherent in the fiction, is the less likely outcome (or, at least, only as likely as the evil outcome."[6] Carroll, that is, thinks audiences root for the *moral* outcome. But I think not always. Someone may prefer the non-moral outcome and still feel suspense. Dracula is being pursued by a group of vampire hunters. He is very powerful, true, but the vampire hunters are also very determined, and in any case, it is nearly dawn. Neither you nor I know whether Dracula will be killed for good. We both care about what happens next, and so are in suspense. But you prefer that Dracula be destroyed forever (the morally correct outcome), while I prefer that he escape (not the morally correct outcome—or maybe the moral values in the typical tales of Dracula are ambivalent, presenting us both with Dracula's murderous deeds as well as his sophistication, erotic appeal, and of course his cool, supernatural powers).

Sometimes, then, we have a preference for the morally correct outcome, sometimes a preference for the morally incorrect outcome (we root for the thief to get away or for Dracula to elude his hunters). This might mean our need to know outcomes is based on some sympathy for characters, quite apart from whether those characters are morally worthy of our sympathy. But even this much need not always hold. There are narratives that fill me with suspense though I don't have sympathy with any of their characters—I think here of the film *The Hunt for Red October*. Too, the mystery story does not typically arouse suspense through sympathy with the murderee or antipathy toward one of the suspects. It may be that the very nature of a plot, which seems always to portend some further development (until, that is, the climax) hooks suspense onto natural human curiosity. As Scheherezade realized, told the beginning of the story its audience naturally wants to know the outcome.

---

6. Noël Carroll, *The Philosophy of Horror* (New York: Routledge, 1990), 137–38.

Carroll thought that suspense is aroused only if the preferred outcome is implied as less likely than the alternatives. I think the *strongest* cases of suspense may do that: they are narratives that make it appear more likely than not that the protagonist with whom we sympathize will be caught or killed or whatever. But there are narratives that don't imply the lessened likelihood of our preferred outcome. In Jacques Demy's *Umbrellas of Cherbourg*, Genevieve and Guy, lovers briefly, are separated by war. Genevieve, who has given birth to her and Guy's daughter, and urged by her mother, marries another man. Guy returns from the war, marries Madeleine, has a son by her, and opens a service station with money left to him by his aunt. Of course, as we know she would, Genevieve eventually drives into the service station with their daughter. What will Guy do? Now the narrative makes it seem fifty-fifty at this point whether Guy will stay with Madeleine or leave with Genevieve. I rooted for Madeleine. Yet I felt suspense nonetheless. (As it happens, Guy tells Genevieve that it would be better if she left immediately, which she does.)

Third, suspense would seem to be aroused only when we are ignorant or uncertain of the outcome. One solution to the paradox denies (S1)— denies that uncertainty is a necessary condition for experiencing suspense.[7] This seems to me entirely unconvincing, as it is precisely when we know everything there is to know about a situation that we do not feel suspense. We wait for the results of the surgery in a state of high suspense. "The waiting is the worst," we say. "If only I knew what was going on." And the feelings of discomfort are somewhat alleviated when the surgeon gives us a good report—he removes our uncertainty and with it the pain of not knowing. But now the paradox comes forward. If suspense requires a need to know what happened next, and if that need is satisfied, how then can one feel suspense?

Simulacra of Ignorance

The most promising solutions to the paradox of suspense try to provide some simulacrum of ignorance of a narrative's outcome. In effect, each

---

7. I refer to a paper by Harold Skulsky, who writes of Walton's quasi-uncertainty, "The mistake here . . . is to assume any essential connection between suspense and uncertainty." Harold Skulsky, "On Being Moved by Fiction," *Journal of Aesthetics and Art Criticism* 39 (1980): 13.

solves the paradox of suspense by denying (S3) through affirming that there is a sort of uncertainty about outcomes present in the repeater's experience. These simulacra of ignorance produce suspense, though what these simulacra are and how they operate varies from theory to theory.

Richard Gerrig refers to the paradox of suspense as "anomalous suspense"—anomalous because the repeater seems to lack access to information he clearly possesses. Why? Gerrig claims that "because time is unidirectional . . . every experience is unique," and consequently "in our everyday lives . . . we have incorporated an *expectation of uniqueness* into the cognitive processes that guide our experience of the world."

> When we read a text for the second time, we are violating the general constraint on non-repetition. Anomalous suspense and anomalous replotting arise because the system acts in ignorance of these violations. We can make an analogy to perceptual illusions. Under special circumstances, our perceptual system can be made to fail. The failures require no special explanation. Anomalous suspense and anomalous replotting can be thought of as cognitive illusions. . . .
>
> Even when certain knowledge of (often undesirable) outcomes intrudes on the experience of a text, the reader continues to consider all outcomes as possible.[8]

This view, as I understand it, suggests that there are two conflicting systems of cognition at work in anomalous suspense, one from our everyday experience, the other from our re-encounters with narrative:

Everyday cognition: We expect every event to be "unique."

Re-encountering narratives: We know what the outcome is.

The expectation of "uniqueness" is Gerrig's simulacrum of ignorance. As I understand it, his view says that our everyday interactions with the ordinary factual world saddle us with the expectation that every event will be "unique," an expectation so hard to shake that it continues to operate even when we re-encounter narratives whose outcomes we might know

---

8. Richard J. Gerrig, "Reexperiencing Fiction and Non-Fiction," *Journal of Aesthetics and Art Criticism* 47 (1989): 279.

quite well. The expectation of uniqueness can't be shaken, and continues to operate. It is as if ordinary life delivered to us constant experiences of yellowness, yet every once in a while we encountered situations we knew weren't yellow, though still they looked yellow. Or more to the point: Everyday life on Gerrig's view is constantly surprising, so much so that we can't shake off the expectation of surprise even when we repeat a story we know well. Anomalous suspense is an illusion in the sense that our expectation of uniqueness only makes us *think* we don't quite know what's coming next when we in fact do.

There are two problems with Gerrig's view. Even if there were an expectation of uniqueness, why shouldn't this inform other aspects of life (other than narratives)? I visit my old aunt. Our visits are always the same. I ask after her health, we sit down for tea, she asks me about my teaching, I ask her if she needs anything, we say good-bye. But I never feel as if I am in suspense over what will happen next, though one might expect that an expectation of uniqueness would infect my visits to my aunt and leave me in "suspense" over what comes next.

The second problem is that events in the world are not as "unique" as Gerrig needs to establish the "expectation of uniqueness" that informs our re-encounters with narratives. We can often predict what will happen next. Milk tastes like milk, the car starts when we turn the key, winter brings cold, and so on. I think Gerrig may have arrived at expectations of uniqueness through an ambiguity in "unique." I may have started my car a hundred times and exactly the same thing happens each time so in one sense each start is not unique at all. In another sense each start is unique in that it is numerically distinct from all other starts. This latter sense is sometimes called numerical distinctness. But two things that are numerically distinct (unique in that sense) may still share all or nearly all other physical properties. Each ping-pong ball in a bag of one hundred is in one sense unique, that is, numerically distinct from each other ball, but in another sense not unique for one ball is pretty much the same as another.

The metaphysics of identity aside, when I start my car I do *not* expect a unique event to occur. I expect the same thing to happen as happened ninety-nine times before: that is, I expect today's start to differ from earlier starts only numerically. And if there is any general expectation with which we approach the world, it is the expectation of *sameness* (which is why Hume wanted to think of induction as a *habit*). Surprise is an infrequent not a constant feature of cognition. Thus Gerrig has little uncertainty from daily life to inject into our experience of repeated narratives, hence no solution to the paradox.[9]

Kendall Walton proposes a solution to the paradox based on his theory of make-believe. Charles engages in an imaginative exercise in which he makes-believe that he is about to be engulfed by a (cinematic) slime, and thereby experiences quasi-fear. Repeaters also engage in imaginative exercises. The repeater who knows that Alicia and Devlin get away with their wine cellar escapade, engages according to Walton in an imaginative exercise in which he makes-believe that he is *un*certain. The repeater must not only make-believe that he is spectator as Alicia and Devlin are in the wine cellar; he also makes-believe that as witness he does not know the outcome. The result of the latter act of imagination is (quasi) suspense. It is fictionally true though factually false that the repeater does not know what comes next in the narrative. "'What readers know' is ambiguous," Walton claims, "between what they 'know' qua participants in their games of make-believe and what they know qua observers of a fictional world . . . between what it is fictional that they know and what they know to be fictional."[10] This suggests a biplanal view of cognitive mental activity with regard to appreciating fiction:

Fictional plane: Pretended or make-believe ignorance as to whether the spies are caught produces (quasi) suspense.

Factual plane: Actual knowledge that the spies are not caught precludes (actual) suspense.

Can a person make-believe ignorance of p when he in fact knows that p, and thereby feel suspense? Now I do not mean to ask whether a person can, as we might say, pretend uncertainty. Of course we can do that. Suppose I am invited to lunch by President Clinton, who launches into an anecdote which, it turns out, I've heard many times before. I know all its twists and turns. Still, during the story I sit in rapt attention, giving out little calculated gasps of excitement; and at its conclusion I say,

9. In a reply to an earlier version of this chapter that was published in the *British Journal of Aesthetics* in 1996, Gerrig seems to change his views. "Anomalous suspense," he writes, "does not rely on an accidental retrieval failure. Rather, it reflects a systematic failure of memory processes to produce relevant knowledge as a narrative unfolds." Richard J. Gerrig, "Is There a Paradox of Suspense? A Reply to Yanal," *British Journal of Aesthetics* 37 (1997): 172. With this I have no quarrel, since if we can't remember what happens next in a narrative, though we may have previously seen the movie or read the book, then we are in ignorance of its outcome, and suspense is possible.

10. Walton, *Mimesis as Make-Believe*, 270.

"What a story, Mr. President. You had me on the edge of my seat!" Now I was no more uncertain about the outcome of the story than I was in suspense. My response is entirely false, feigned, mimed (though, one hopes, forgivable). Nor do I mean to ask whether a person can momentarily be unable to recollect (and in that sense be ignorant of) that which he knows. I mean: Can a person who actively knows the outcome also and at the same time maintain a make-believe ignorance sufficient to generate feelings of suspense?

Walton presents his solution to the paradox of suspense on a par with his solution to the paradox of emotion and fiction. That is, he thinks both (A) and (B) to be similar exercises in make-belief.

(A) Jay makes-believe that the spies are in grave danger and Jay thereby feels (quasi) apprehension for their safety. Jay believes that there are no spies in any danger.

(B) Jay makes-believe that he is uncertain of the outcome in the wine cellar, and he thereby feels (quasi) suspense. Jay knows clearly that the spies are not found out.

However there is a significant difference between (A) and (B). In order for it to remain just a game of make-believe for Jay, his belief that there are no spies (i.e., that *Notorious* is "just a story") must *somehow* continue to operate and exert some influence on his game, else make-belief becomes belief and Jay finds himself treating *Notorious* as docudrama. If the children forget that stumps aren't really bears, their game of running from stumps becomes all too real. Yet it would seem that for suspense to be generated by the game described in (B), there cannot be any interaction between the fictional and factual planes. Jay's game of making-believe that he doesn't know the outcome cannot be infiltrated by his knowledge of that outcome. This would promptly squelch suspense in the fictional plane. So the factual and fictional planes cannot intersect when (B) is played. But this seems an exception simply to save the theory.

Noël Carroll advocates a thought-theoretic solution to the paradox of suspense. Carroll claims that suspense can take hold only if the audience believes the outcome is uncertain, though at the same time "the audience may entertain the thought that the relevant outcome is uncertain or improbable."[11] Kay who re-views *Notorious* and feels suspense would then be simultaneously in these two mental states:

11. Carroll, "The Paradox of Suspense," 87.

Kay entertains the thought (imagines) that she is uncertain whether the spies are found out.

Kay knows that the spies are not found out.

Carroll's solution is similar to Walton's but relies on the structurally simpler activity of entertaining in thought.

Simplicity aside, for Kay to feel suspense (over the spies' fate) her suspense must not only be generated by her imagination; it must remain uninfected by what she knows. I do not wish to say that this is impossible— I think it is in a sense possible—but it requires more explanation than Carroll gives. Even if there is a "split" between what we imagine and what we know, we have no assurance that emotion will be sparked by imagination unimpeded by knowledge. Isn't there, when Kay both imagines that she is uncertain of the outcome and also knows it, at least a fifty-fifty chance that Kay's affects will "side with" her knowledge of the scene's outcome, and therefore that she won't feel suspense?

The Inactivation of Recollection

If repeaters do re-experience suspense as the paradox of suspense holds, then the solution will not be found in a simulacrum of ignorance piled on top of recollection of that outcome. We might borrow an idea from Thought Theory T. To the extent a repeater can inactivate (put out of mind) his recollection of what happens next, he can thereby put himself into a state of (temporary) ignorance about a narrative's outcome. This is not a simulacrum of ignorance but real though induced temporary ignorance. It is like forcing oneself not to think of something, an act of will that can sometimes succeed. This temporary ignorance may be sufficient for enabling feelings of suspense.

How is recollection to be inactivated? If thought theory is in general correct then the spectator to fictional narrative is caught up in thoughts of characters and situations. He may well be so distracted by these thoughts that his powers of recollection are put on hold. The repeater knows the outcome but may not recollect it if he is highly focused on what he entertains in thought. If we can, as Theory T holds, inactivate our disbeliefs in the fictionality of a narrative's characters, we should be able to inactivate our recollection of the outcomes to their various exploits.

However, it is, I think, more difficult to inactivate recollection of outcomes that to inactivate disbelief in the fictionality of characters. Fictional characters very rarely prod us to acknowledge their fictionality. With certain modernist exceptions, fiction maintains the illusion of reality. But one incident in a narrative we know well can easily trigger recollection of what comes next. Consider a repeater's experience as he watches *King Kong*. He comes to the scene in which Kong is chained on the stage of the huge auditorium. The flash bulbs go off and Kong becomes increasingly agitated, and then. . . . This repeater if he is to experience suspense must now inactivate his recollection of what comes next. Yet his recollection that Kong breaks his chains and escapes into the streets of New York may well already be triggered. The inactivation of recollection is thus harder to maintain than the inactivation of disbelief in fictionality, for there are few fictional stories in which characters remind us of their fictionality.

I do not take the difficulties in inactivating recollection to be tragic, for there are advantages for repeaters to allow themselves to recollect away. True, they thereby forego suspense, but perhaps gain other experiences in exchange. Suspense is an emotion that tends to overwhelm all others. Suspense makes one nearly oblivious to anything else. But fiction, even when it offers suspense, often offers much more.

A first time viewer of *Casablanca* will be in suspense during the final scene at the airport. Will Ilsa Lund (Ingrid Bergman) leave with her husband, Victor Laszlo (Paul Henreid), or will she stay with her true love, Rick (Humphrey Bogart)? Since suspense is such a strong emotion, the first time viewer may be so fixated on it that he misses other aspects of the film. The repeater who has seen the film many times and who actively recollects that Ilsa will board that airplane, leaving Rick and Luis (Claude Rains), the police prefect, to start their "beautiful friendship," is perhaps better able to feel a little bit in love with Bergman, to admire Bogart for his ironic altruism, to be humored by Claude Rains's order (having just shot Major Strasser) to "round up the usual suspects." Such a repeater will revel in the romantic fatalism of the events of *Casablanca*, something quite possibly not felt by the first-time viewer who is still in suspense over what comes next.

Indeed, it is recollection of outcomes and not suspense that informs much of our re-experience of narrative. Just about everyone who has seen Alfred Hitchcock's *Psycho* (1960) knows that Marion Crane (Janet Leigh) is murdered in the shower, in a masterful sequence, possibly the most famous every put on celluloid. (Could anyone who has seen this sequence inactivate his recollection of it?) The first time viewer of *Psycho* will be in slight suspense about whether Marion (Janet Leigh) will get away with the money she has stolen. The first time viewer is not concerned about her *physical* safety. All the first time viewer knows is that Marion has stolen a large sum of money from her boss's client, driven off, and checked into the old Bates Motel. She has been given a room next to the motel office, in which she has a chat with the odd, shy young proprietor, Norman Bates (Anthony Perkins). Returning to her room, Marion begins to undress, while next door Norman Bates moves a picture to peek at her through a hole in the wall. The first time viewer will sense that Marion is not in an especially wholesome situation (and, of course, she's on the lam). The first time viewer has no strong apprehension about Marion's fate, because he doesn't know of the murder in the shower. Hitchcock doesn't signal that murder, say, by making Norman Bates more threatening. Marion's murder is, if anything, not even in the cards given that the film isn't half over and she is its main character.

As Marion undresses and steps into the shower, the repeater who recollects what is about to happen feels something that I would like to call fear of the known. The recollecting repeater is not in suspense about Marion's fate, for he knows exactly what that fate is. Such a repeater is strongly apprehensive on Marion's behalf—his horror mounts as she enters the tub and turns on the shower—precisely because he knows that she is about to be brutally stabbed to death. Apprehensiveness and mounting horror are not suspense, though they can occur together (as when we are apprehensive because we are in suspense).

Were any of the simulacrum theorists discussed earlier correct, the recollecting repeater who re-views *Psycho* would be on each successive screening, in suspense over what happens to Marion. As she steps into the shower, the recollecting repeater would on some level know but on another level not know what happens next. According to a simulacrum theorist, a repeater does not feel a sense of apprehension or mounting horror—even of quasi-apprehension or quasi-mounting-horror—for the recollecting repeater is forever slightly suspenseful over what comes next. But this seems quite false to our repetitions of *Psycho*, and indeed many other narratives. Why else are the novels of Robert Ludlum, Tom Clancy, Frederick Forsyth, and others, which have little to offer their readers apart from the thrill of suspense, much read but not much re-read?

The Forward-Looking Emotions

The pervasiveness of suspense during repeated viewings is, I think, overstated. It may take a few viewings or readings before a repeater can confidently say that he recollects a narrative's twists and turns of plot. Sometimes a repeater will know the bare outlines of the outcome. A re-viewer of *Notorious* may recollect that Cary Grant and Ingrid Bergman *somehow* are not given away during their search in the "wine cellar," though he may not recollect exactly how. There is no paradox in feeling suspense over how the details within a narrative sequence, even if one correctly remembers the general outcome. (This may account for the suspense Gerrig feels from reading about the making of the atom bomb. Though he of course knows that the bomb is eventually made, he may feel suspense because he is uncertain of the steps in between.)

But Carroll claims suspense even in his fiftieth viewing of *King Kong*. Walton, Gerrig, and others would agree. Are repeaters really working so hard and constantly at inactivating recollection? Is repeated *suspense* really so pervasive? I think not.

In Andrew Bergman's 1990 film, *The Freshman*, Clark Kellogg (Matthew Broderick) enrolls in New York University's film school, where his professor (Paul Benedict) discusses, in minute detail, Francis Ford Coppola's 1972 *The Godfather*. (One of the jokes in *The Freshman* comes when Kellogg is offered a job by one Carmine Sabatini, played by Marlon Brando reprising his *Godfather* role.) While clips from *The Godfather* are being screened for his class, the professor watches from the back of the room, mouthing the lines along with the screen actors. Is such a repeater really in suspense over whether the Hollywood mogul Jack Woltz (John Marley) will eventually give the movie role to Johnny Fontane (Al Martino)? Of course not. The professor knows the film inside out. He knows that the Corleones will make Woltz an offer he can't refuse, an offer Woltz finds in his silk-sheeted, blood-soaked bed. In Walton's example, Lauren has heard the story of Jack and the Beanstalk over and over again; and yet she feels suspense over and over. Lauren doesn't forget in between. Nor does she inactivate her recollections (no thought theorist, Walton). Lauren is a repeater who nonetheless, as Walton has it, feels suspense. Or does she?

Now, not everything that can be described is thereby possible, though it can be made to seem so. Suppose I describe a case in which a person wanders about disembodied. The fact that such a case can be rendered with plausibility—it is, in fact, the core plot of films from *Topper* to *Ghost*—

doesn't mean that it is thereby a *possible* case, and that materialism is thereby disproved. Disembodied persons may well be *impossibilities*, though convincingly, sometimes charmingly, portrayed in narrative. Now Walton's example does little more than describe with disarming simplicity a case of someone who recollects the outcome of a narrative, yet who is said to feel suspense. I maintain that we need more than a description here; we need an *argument* that Lauren's mental state is possible.

Walton might maintain that there are arguments to this effect all around us. Look at the way children want a story re-told. Look at the adults who view *Casablanca* over and over. Well, yes, but what does this show? It doesn't, at least off the top, show that such people are both certain of the outcome and filled with suspense. It might show something rather different, namely that stories and movies have more to offer than simple suspense at their outcomes. Lauren might enjoy hearing the tale because it is familiar and familiarity is itself a comfort; or because daddy is paying such nice attention to her; or because she loves the part where the beans grow so high. Walton himself provides a variety of responses Lauren might have: admiration for Jack's exploits, the "thrill of adventure," and so on, though of course none of these are or are contingent on suspense. Lauren might well recollect that the giant threatening Jack is killed when Jack cuts the beanstalk out from under him; but she may still experience fear when Jack is threatened, for the thoughts she is entertaining are threatening thoughts (thoughts of threatening situations). But experiencing fear is neither itself suspense nor is it contingent on ignorance. (I may know with certainty that my friend will be executed tomorrow, and yet feel fear for him, anxiety over his welfare, etc.)

What, then, of Carroll's testimony that he feels suspense on seeing *King Kong* for the fiftieth time? Shouldn't we take him at his word? Not necessarily. There is, I think, a reason why it sometimes *seems* that repeaters re-experience suspense. They may confuse suspense with something else. Lauren, for example, is said to worry about Jack's fate, and to be filled with excitement when she hears of his exploits. But one can worry about what one knows will happen (the test tomorrow, death, taxes). One can also be filled with excitement over what one correctly anticipates (vacation begins tomorrow). Neither worry nor excitement requires ignorance of an outcome, though worry or excitement often accompanies suspense.

However, there is a way in which the repeater's experience picks up certain qualities such as anticipation or apprehension that are forward-looking emotions like suspense and thus perhaps confused with suspense.

The repeater looks forward with anticipation to the airport farewell in *Casablanca*; or he apprehensively waits for the shower murder in *Psycho*; or he is excited that he will get to see King Kong climb once again to the top of the Empire State Building. Such a repeater may be tempted to say he is in suspense, but if suspense is an emotion grounded in ignorance of the outcome and if one actively recollects that outcome, then one has misidentified anticipation or apprehension or excitement as suspense.

We can easily go wrong with a prima facie answer to the question, What emotion am I feeling? The prima facie answer goes first for the gross contours of the "raw feel" of the emotion. An emotion may feel pleasurable or discomfiting to us, and its hedonistic quality can deliver a prima facie identification. But then we may say we feel joy when we really feel hope or that we feel fear when we really feel mistrust. A feeling that wells up very strongly may be felt as happiness though it induces tears. And I think suspense can be misidentified. We may initially seize on the forward- or backward-looking contours of an emotion. But now anticipation may appear as suspense, or grief as regret. On second thought, the prima facie answer may be corrected: we think the situation through a bit more, we identify the intentional object of the emotion, and so on. We often "reason out" what emotion we are properly feeling.

It is, I suggest, the prima facie *mis*identification of emotions that now and again creates the *appearance* of suspense in recollecting repeaters. When Janet Leigh's Marion enters that shower in *Psycho*, a repeater might report that he is in suspense over what happens, though this might well be a misidentification of something else: his apprehension for Marion's fate. When the recollecting repeater once again views *Sleepless in Seattle*, he might say he is in suspense over whether Annie Reed (Meg Ryan) will keep her rendezvous at the top of the Empire State Building with Sam Baldwin (Tom Hanks), though the truth may be that our recollecting repeater is in a state of anticipation: he looks forward to the romantic satisfaction afforded by a scene he enjoys.

Why are emotions other than suspense easily re-experienced by repeat viewers and readers? The simple answer is: We can re-experience any emotion that does not require ignorance. Walton quotes Leonard Bernstein, "I've seen [*West Side Story*] about five thousand times maybe. And I always end up in tears."[12] Walton prefaces this to his discussion of suspense, but the quote is not quite on point. Bernstein's reaction (it might be better to

12. Walton, *Mimesis as Make-Believe*, 259.

say his *stamina*) is certainly true of some who re-experience narrative: some are always, over and over again, delighted to see Meg Ryan and Tom Hanks finally connect, excited as Kong climbs the Empire State Building, anxious over Janet Leigh's shower, and appalled at Desdemona's murder. We can infer, at least, that such emotions don't require ignorance, and accordingly can go on in the full knowledge of what comes next. There must be times when a plot is so ingrained in one's mind that one *couldn't* inactivate knowledge of its outcome. Surely, Bernstein did not five thousand times experience *suspense* over whether Tony dies at the end of *West Side Story*.

the paradox
of tragedy

In Aristotle's classic formulation, the spectators of tragedy should be brought to feel pity and fear for the tragic hero. Now pity and fear are what are sometimes termed negative emotions, that is emotions that are not pleasant to experience. Negative emotions abound in our experience of fiction. Horror movies arouse terror or disgust; the unjust treatment of fictional characters can arouse anger; stories of loss (lost loves, youth, pets) can bring on feelings of deep sadness; even suspense, the subject of the previous chapter, is an uncomfortable emotion. And yet stories that arouse the negative emotions are consumed by the bushel. Even if classic tragedy remains a highbrow taste, masses flock to horror movies and weepies (as the enormous box office success of *Titanic* has demonstrated).

There is a puzzle looming here, classically called the paradox of tragedy, though the puzzle embraces more than tragedy narrowly construed (our enjoyment of horror stories calls up virtually the same paradox, for example). How to begin the paradox is, however, disputed. It would be simplest to assert that the negative emotions are painful, but as Kendall Walton points out, "Sometimes we like [feeling emotions like sorrow and terror] and sometimes we don't."[1] Still, it is true that some fictional characters and situations arouse *unpleasant* pity, sorrow, fear, disgust, and the like. We might on occasion avoid tragic stories simply because we want something more uniformly pleasant. So the paradox begins with this apparent truth:

(T1) Certain emotions toward fiction (including pity, sorrow, fear, and disgust) are negative (unpleasant).

And yet people *enjoy* these experiences. "It's so sad that Jack Dawson dies near the end of *Titanic*, but I loved the movie. I've seen it three times already." Or, "Dracula is such a terrifying character. I'm a real fan of vampire movies." Thus it seems a fact that:

(T2) Spectators enjoy fictions that arouse negative emotions.

Yet how can this be so in face of what is an apparent conceptual truth?

(T3) What is unpleasant cannot be enjoyed.

Two main lines of solution have been proposed. One, which denies (T1), holds that emotions toward fiction are never negative. The control theorists, Marcia Eaton and John Morreall, advocate such a solution (and some commentators put Hume in this camp). The second finds an ambiguity in (T2), holding that while we do not enjoy the negative emotions as such, the circumstances of fictional narratives provide *additional* sources of enjoyment. The meta-response theorists, Susan Feagin and Kendall Walton, posit a satisfaction in feeling pity. Noël Carroll finds a kind of satisfaction in learning things from horror stories. I also argue that Hume falls in this camp as well, holding that there are additional pleasures to be had from the aesthetic qualities of the fictional narrative. Sometimes the first kind of solution is called a "conversion" theory, and the second a "combination" theory. I argue for a combination theory, though at the end, suggest that a combination theory must be supplemented by Thought Theory T.

1. Kendall Walton, *Mimesis as Make-Believe* (Ithaca: Cornell University Press, 1990), 256.

The Controlled Emotion and Pleasure

Marcia Eaton and John Morreall have held that there is something about the situation wherein we read or view works of art that lends "control" to our emotions; and it is this control that diverts the unpleasantness of the negative emotions. The form of control theories is basically this: Some set of circumstances is said to enable us to be in control of our emotions, negative or otherwise; and control is then said to enable emoters to take pleasure in (or at least not to feel displeasure from) any negative emotions. What control theorists will affirm is that negative emotions are unpleasant only in uncontrolled situations, and reading a book or viewing a play is a controlled situation. It is control that diverts the potential pain from the negative emotions.

Here is Marcia Eaton on control:

> A horror story is fun to read only when we are in control of the situation in which we read it. . . . Often recognition that what we are reading, watching, hearing, etc. is "unreal" is enough to assure us that we are "in control." . . . We do no enjoy a roller coaster which is "out of control," but only one which we believe will stay on the track and stop at the appointed time and place.
>
> In controlled surroundings, tragedy permits us to purge ourselves of bottled-up feelings. Indeed we seek out tragedies . . . in the belief that a controlled experience will excite, enrich, purge, and/or sensitize us in certain ways, and we take genuine pleasure in this experience. . . .
>
> When we are what I have loosely called "in control" we can formulate and consider descriptions of objects and actions or events which we do not find ourselves able to formulate or consider when we lack control.[2]

Eaton claims two independent sufficient conditions for being in control. If you feel "safe" you're in control of your emotions (the roller coaster example). Or, if you're of the presence of mind so that you can "formulate and consider descriptions of object of emotion" you're in control.

Yet a person safe and sound by the side of the road will behold with *painful* horror the carnage of a terrible auto accident that doesn't involve him. And a person trembling in his boots while being robbed at gunpoint

---

2. Marcia Eaton, "A Strange Sort of Sadness," *Journal of Aesthetics and Art Criticism* 41 (1982): 59, 60.

is later able to provide the police a detailed and accurate description of his assailant, though he also tells us later that he was sick from fear. The problem is not that Eaton doesn't put forth two plausible sufficient conditions for what we might call "being in control"; it is rather that being in control in those ways doesn't necessarily remove the pain from the negative emotions.

John Morreall sets out another control theory:

> [W]e can enjoy negative emotions only when we retain our overall control of our situation. . . .
>
> It is usually easiest to maintain control . . . when we are merely attending to something that has no practical consequences for us. Then being in control requires only the abilities to start, stop, and direct our attention and thought. By contrast, when the situation evoking the negative emotion has practical consequences, especially when it requires action from us, it is unlikely that we will feel in control. . . . Now most of the time when we feel negative emotions toward fiction, and much of the time when we feel such emotions toward the past, we experience the control mentioned above, of attending to something which has no practical consequences for us, and being able to start, stop, and direct this attending. . . .
>
> In real life our emotions often get too strong to be enjoyable, but in fiction this is far less likely. . . . Part of the artist's job is to present that situation in such a way that we can stay in control while feeling negative emotions, so that we can get satisfaction from the experience, rather than being overwhelmed and utterly distressed by it. We feel that the artist has slipped up if the fictional work is, say, so graphic in its depiction of violence or suffering that most of the audience is disgusted and has to stop reading the book or watching the movie screen.[3]

Morreall presents three apparently independent sufficient conditions for having control: If the situation holds no "practical consequences" for us; or if we are able to "start, stop, and direct" attention to it; or if the emotion it inspires is not "too strong"; then we will be in control of that emotion; and given our control, any emotion we will have will be pain-free.

In Morreall's discussion, practical situations demand action; so non-practical situations must be, by inference, those that do not demand action. Spectators know they cannot assist fictional characters. Hence

---

3. John Morreall, "Enjoying Negative Emotions in Fictions," *Philosophy and Literature* 9 (1985): 97, 101.

reading a novel or watching a film will be the very paradigm of a nonpractical situation. But of course, there are situations apart from fictional narratives which verge on what Morreall means by the nonpractical: for example, we hear about a massacre that takes place in Bosnia, which causes us to be angry with the perpetrators; we read about a fire that kills two children, and we pity their parents. Perhaps in some saintly sense these situations demand action, though most people will experience them as cases in which nothing can be done. Will their anger or pity be denuded of unpleasantness just because (they believe) nothing can be done? I see no argument that it will, and further, an argument in the other direction: situations that cannot be undone might inspire *harsher* anger, or *more poignant* pity.

I say that these situation *verge* on the kind of impracticality associated with our relation to fictions. Admittedly we *could* intervene in Bosnia in a way that we *can't* intervene in *King Lear*. We could write letters to our congressman, stage protest rallies, and fly to Bosnia to join the Red Cross, and so on—but obviously letters and rallies can't stop Lear's two daughters from their murderous and ungrateful designs. In any event, how will a sense that a situation does not demand or in some way inhibits action eliminate pain from negative emotions? The only way to connect nonpracticality with painlessness is to hold that the pain in the negative emotions is brought on when the emoter anticipates acting. Eliminate the anticipation of action, and you will eliminate the pain. The pain is, then, somehow in the anticipation of (or demand for) action. But this can't be right because of the existence of certain positive emotions (hope, joy, love) which demand or anticipate action. The lover wants to drive all night to be with his beloved the following day. Is his love by dint of its demands for action painful love? Not necessarily; the lover may take great pleasure in his love's demands.

The ability to stop and start attention is prominent in our experience of fiction. We can put the book down, voluntarily and at any time, though we can't always extricate ourselves from painful situations at will. We might be bound by duty to the deathbed of a loved one, though we are not bound by anything to continue reading a novel that includes a deathbed scene. Morreall thinks that because of our stop-and-start ability—I'll call it our voluntary participation—we will enjoy our sorrow over the fictional deathbed scene, though we will not enjoy our sorrow at the deathbed of a loved one. Yet Morreall himself reminds us that sometimes we put a book down precisely because it arouses emotions that are too strong, the implication being that we sometimes begin to experience painful feelings even given our voluntary participation. And any account that connects voluntary participation with painlessness must imply that it is involuntary participation that puts the pain in the emotion. On Morreall's theory, it isn't the fear of the gunman who's robbing that makes the experience so unpleasant so much as the fact that we can't just walk away of our own volition. Imagine, though, that the doors on a move theater have been jammed shut by an avalanche thereby trapping an audience inside. The theater is playing, as it happens, *A Fish Called Wanda*. Morreall's theory predicts that their emotional responses will be painful (they can't stop and start their attention); I predict, on the contrary, that they will find their emotional responses to be delightful.

On Morreall's third condition, an emotion that is weak (not too strong) will be controlled and thereby be painless. Certainly if you turn down the volume on fear you will turn down its discomfort. But Morreall wants to maintain something more: not just that a weakly felt fear will be slightly unpleasant, but that a weakly felt fear will not be unpleasant at all. Hume in his essay on the tragic paradox disagrees: "You may by degrees weaken a real sorrow, till it totally disappears; yet in none of its gradations will it ever give pleasure; except, perhaps, by accident, to a man sunk under lethargic indolence, whom it rouses from that languid state."[4]

Maybe, though, Hume is wrong. Maybe fear and the other negative emotions need a pain threshold, so that a weakly felt fear (or repulsion or pity) doesn't quite feel uncomfortable (yet). But for such a claim to solve the tragic paradox it must further be true that *all* negative emotions generated by interaction with fiction are weakly felt. This is on its face false, for we often *profoundly* feel sorrow or anger toward fictions. But how then will we explain the fact that we enjoy these very fictions?

Control theories founder on another fact. There is pleasure to be had from *losing* control. One man controls his anger at his boss. He checks his words, puts a smile on his face, clenches his fists (though where his boss won't see them); he speaks light-heartedly and matter-of-factly. This does not paint a picture of a pain-free experience—the very opposite in fact. Another gives vent to his rage: he raises his voice, bangs on the desk, disparages his boss's management style—and enjoys himself enormously, though perhaps to his later regret.

---

4. David Hume, "Of Tragedy," originally published in *Four Dissertations* (1757). Cited here as reprinted in Stephen Copley and Andrew Edgar, eds., *David Hume: Selected Essays* (New York: Oxford University Press, 1993), 33.

Meta-Responses, Learning, and Pleasure

"Direct responses to tragedy are responses to the unpleasantness of the work, and they are hence unpleasant experiences," Susan Feagin writes.[5] In addition, the experience of tragedy also includes what she calls a "meta-response of satisfaction."

> We find ourselves to be the kind of people who respond negatively to villainy, treachery, and injustice. This discovery, or reminder, is something which, quite justly, yields satisfaction. In a way it shows what we care for, and in showing we care for the welfare of human beings and that we deplore the immoral forces that defeat them, it reminds us of our common humanity. It reduces one's sense of aloneness in the world, and soothes, psychologically, the pain of solipsism.[6]

Kendall Walton at one point adumbrates a similar theory: "Given that [Anna Karenina] suffers as she does, it would seem fitting and appropriate, the least one can do, to pay attention to her predicament and to grieve for her. One may feel satisfaction amidst one's tears in doing this much."[7] However he extends Feagin's idea just a bit more, holding that there may be times when "One may *want* to experience sorrow, and may find a certain enjoyment or satisfaction in the fact that one does experience it."[8] True, but we must look closely at what has been enjoyed. Suppose a person spends a day at the beach, and he tells us he enjoyed his day very much. He reports that during the day he played in the surf, ate hot dogs and French-fries, had a delightful conversation with a person he met, but stubbed his toe on a sharp rock. Now in saying he enjoyed his day, we should not infer that he took pleasure in every aspect of his day. It is unlikely that he enjoyed stubbing his toe on a sharp rock. So too when a person reports that he enjoyed having a good cry, he might mean that before his cry he had a sense of emotional ill-being, and that after he had a pleasurable sense of emotional release. He *needn't* mean that he enjoyed the cry (or sadness) itself.

5. Susan Feagin, "The Pleasures of Tragedy," *American Philosophical Quarterly* 20 (1983): 97.
6. Feagin, "The Pleasures of Tragedy," 98. Feagin discusses other cases of meta-response (e.g., being disturbed by taking pleasure in reading a sadomasochistic novel) in her *Reading With Feeling* (Ithaca: Cornell University Press, 1996), 130–31.
7. Walton, *Mimesis as Make-Believe*, 257.
8. All quotes in this section are from Walton, *Mimesis as Make-Believe*, 256 and 257.

It seems to me that we do, sometimes, feel pleasure because we have been able to respond emotionally to another's suffering. And it seems plausible to hold, as Feagin and Walton do, that there is pleasure attendant upon such self-congratulation. Does this solve the paradox? Remember that we want to explain how someone can assert, truly, that he *enjoyed* last night's performance of *King Lear*, though he felt negative pity, horror, and disgust. The meta-response of satisfaction cannot prevent or efface any unpleasantness attendant on our pity, for our pity for Lear must be felt *before* we take satisfaction in feeling, and the future cannot prevent or erase the past. The question then becomes: Is the meta-response of satisfaction sufficiently pleasant to counterbalance any negativity from our pity, disgust, and the rest, so that we have a overall sense of enjoyment? Perhaps on occasion it is, but my sense is that we should seek further sources of satisfaction.

But there is also this issue: The Feagin/Walton suggestion seems to work only for the other-regarding negative emotions: principally pity, but also sadness or anger over another's fate. What of being frightened or disgusted, emotions which are self-regarding? As I understand it, the satisfaction of being the sort of person who feels X is supposed to be a moral satisfaction, or satisfaction in a kind of moral achievement (specifically, feeling something for another's predicament). It isn't simply taking satisfaction in being the sort of person who can have emotions *simpliciter*. It therefore seems out of range of that theory to hold that we have a "meta-response of satisfaction" to being the sort of person who is repelled by a scaly monster or frightened by alien invaders.

According to Noël Carroll, the spectator of a horror story feels various negative emotions—fear, terror, disgust, even repulsion—but nonetheless gains satisfaction through a process of learning:

> The pleasure derived from the horror fiction and the source of our interest in it resides, first and foremost, in the processes of discovery, proof, and confirmation that horror fictions often employ. The disclosure of the existence of the horrific being and of its properties is the central source of pleasure in the genre; once that process of revelation is consummated, we remain inquisitive about whether such a creature can be successfully confronted, and that narrative question sees us through to the end of the story. Here, the pleasure involved is, broadly speaking, cognitive.[9]

9. Nöel Carroll, *The Philosophy of Horror* (New York: Routledge, 1990), 184.

The negative emotions are "part of the price to be paid" for this cognitive pleasure. Our curiosity is piqued by the sheer weirdness of the horrific being—What is it exactly? How can it even be? What can it do? How does it do what it does?—and then satisfied, gradually, through disclosures in the narrative. In Carroll's view, then, the pain or discomfort of the negative emotions aroused by horror stories is not taken away in any sense. Such unpleasantness remains, though we gain a side benefit of having our curiosity aroused and satisfied.

Of course, other (nonhorror) genres of fiction also arouse curiosity, though to be sure over different subject matter. The reader of Jane Austen's *Pride and Prejudice* will be curious as to whether Elizabeth Bennett will accept or reject Mr. Collins's proposal, why Mr. Bingley forsook, without explanation, Jane Bennett, and whether Elizabeth and Darcy will or will not marry. Austen's narrative eventually discloses all. Carroll is aware that other genres also arouse curiosity (though he mentions only the detective thriller), hence bring with them satisfaction of learning something or other. He emphasizes, however, the *special* forms of curiosity aroused by horror stories, especially those populated with kinds of things not found in nature: vampires, body snatchers, spiders as large as houses, zombies, and so on. We're not curious as to how Elizabeth Bennett can sing and play the piano at the same time, for this occurs naturally in the real world. We are, however, curious about how the bodies that arise from the tombs in George Romero's *Night of the Living Dead* can be alive and dead at the same time.

"Learning things is most enjoyable," Aristotle wrote, "not only for philosophers but for others equally."[10] Of course Aristotle meant that learning things about the real world is enjoyable. But I suppose we can be curious and receive satisfaction from "learning" things about the fictional world. The "people" who have risen from the dead in *Night of the Living Dead* are really very scary and repulsive (the film has a reputation for being one of the scariest films ever made). They attack and kill the living, then eat their corpses, right on camera. Ugh! True, the film arouses some curiosity about all this. Who are these people? Escaped maniacs? No, we find out, they're the dead returned to life. Why have they returned to life? We don't know; maybe it's radiation from outer space. What can stop them? They're afraid of fire as it happens. And that's about as far as it

---

10. Aristotle, *Poetics*, IV (1448b), from Aristotle *On Poetry and Style*, trans. G. M. A. Grube (Indianapolis: Hackett Publishing Company, 1987).

goes for learning. We don't find out how "radiation from outer space" brings the dead back to life, nor why they're afraid of fire, nor why they eat the living. The film does not satisfy these curious questions (nor, I think, do we expect it to—horror stories are entertainments, not scientific studies).

Explanations found in most horror stories are similarly minimal. The terrifying happenings in Robert Wise's *The Haunting* receive little more explanation than that the house is crammed with ghosts who are unhappy or evil and who seem to want Eleanor (Julie Harris) for their own. Bram Stoker never gives us a clue how Dracula stays "undead," nor why garlic keeps vampires at bay, nor why being bitten by a vampire transforms the bitten into one, nor why sunlight is bad for the vampire's health. Yet, through our horror and disgust, we still manage to enjoy Dracula. The minimal satisfactions of curiosity, then, don't seem to add up to enough so as to counterbalance the unpleasantness of the negative conditions. So something more than the pleasures of cognition must account for the pleasure we take in horror stories.

David Hume's View

"It seems an unaccountable pleasure which the spectators of a well-written tragedy receive from sorrow, terror, anxiety, and other passions that are in themselves disagreeable and uneasy," Hume wrote in his essay on tragedy ("Of Tragedy," 126). And the unaccountable pleasure occurs not only in well-written tragedies (i.e., fictions). Cicero's "pathetic description of the butchery made by Verres of the Sicilian captains is a masterpiece" which "raised tears in his judges and all his audience [who] were then the most highly delighted, and expressed the greatest satisfaction with the pleader." Being present "at a melancholy scene of that nature" would not "afford any entertainment. Neither is the sorrow here is softened by fiction; for the audience were convinced of the reality of every circumstance" (128).

How then do we take pleasure in narratives that raise "passions disagreeable in themselves"?

I answer: this extraordinary effect proceeds from that very eloquence with which the melancholy scene is represented. The genius required to paint objects in a lively manner, the art employed in collecting all the pathetic circumstances, the judgment displayed in disposing them; the exercise, I say, of these noble talents, together with the force of expression, and beauty of oratorial numbers, diffuse the highest satisfaction on the audience, and excite the most delightful movements. By this means, the uneasiness of the melancholy passions is not only overpowered and effaced by something stronger of an opposite kind, but the whole impulse of those passions is converted into pleasure, and swells the delight which the eloquence raises in us. (128–29)

I take Hume's solution to be a combination view. The negative emotions are "in themselves disagreeable," even when raised by tragedy or Ciceronian oratory. But a representation that is aesthetically apt (eloquent, noble, exciting, beautiful) "excites the most delightful movements" of mind. The beauty and eloquence in the *depiction* of the tragic events cause pleasure sufficient to "overpower" any other unpleasantness. The disagreeableness of the negative emotions becomes part of a "whole impulse" that is pleasurable taken in its entirety, though not entirely devoid of pain.

It is thus the fiction of tragedy softens the passion, by an infusion of a new feeling, not merely by weakening or diminishing the sorrow. You may by degrees weaken a real sorrow, till it totally disappears; yet in none of its gradations will it ever give pleasure; except, perhaps, by accident, to a man sunk under lethargic indolence, whom it rouses from that languid state. (129)

The *sorrow* is not made pleasant, though our overall experience of the tragedy may well be. While we may be tempted to describe our sorrow as pleasant, this would be an error, though an easy mistake to make, given that it is hard to disentangle the various strands of our complex experience of a work of art. We don't think: now I have the pain from my sorrow at the hero's plight, now the pleasure from the beauty of the poet's language. Our only clear impression is of the "bottom line," which is (usually) on balance an overall pleasurable experience. But to hold that the painful sorrow of tragedy has been made pleasant through the addition of the eloquence of the actors and the beauty of the poet's language would be to hold that the coffee itself has lost its bitterness through the addition of sugar and cream.

Some philosophers believe that Hume was a conversion theorist. Mark Packer once referred to Hume's "Conversion Hypothesis," according to which Hume is supposed to have held that the eloquence of the poet's language (and other aesthetic qualities) convert painful pity into pleasant pity.[11] If Hume indeed adopted such a conversion hypothesis, we would have to agree with Susan Feagin who criticizes Hume for not explaining the "mechanics of this conversion."[12] Alex Neill also think Hume maintained a conversion theory of some kind, and cites several places in which Hume speaks of conversions: of how "the whole impulse of these [melancholy] passions is converted into pleasure;" how "the impulse . . . arising from sorrow . . . receives a new direction from the sentiments of beauty;" how the sentiments of beauty "being the predominant emotion, seize the whole mind, and convert the former [the melancholy passions] into themselves, at least tincture them so strongly as totally to alter their nature. And the soul being at the same time roused by passion and charmed by eloquence feels on the whole a strong movement, which is altogether delightful." The pleasure "which poets . . . give us, by exciting grief, sorrow, indignation, compassion is not so . . . paradoxical as it may . . . appear. The force of imagination, the energy of expression, the power of numbers, the charms of imitation; all these are naturally delightful to the mind: and when the object presented lays also hold of some affection, the pleasure still rises upon us, by the conversion of this subordinate movement into that which is predominant."[13]

Neill thinks that to accept the combinatory reading of Hume we have "to find some way . . . of glossing over this talk of conversion."[14] Now it may well be that Hume is running a combination and a conversion theory together in his essay. Certainly in the passages Neill cites Hume clobbers us over the head with the term "conversion." But I think the passages cited in support of a conversion reading of Hume can be seen as consistent with (if not entirely supportive of) a combination reading.

Note that what is said by Hume to be "converted" is a "whole impulse" or the "whole mind" or the "strong movement" the soul "feels on the whole." We find the "movement" of painful emotion undergoing a "conversion" by being "subordinated" into a "predominant" movement by the work's display of "imagination," "energy," "power," and "charm," all of

---

11. Mark Packer, "Dissolving the Paradox of Tragedy," *Journal of Aesthetics and Art Criticism* 47 (1989): 12.

12. Feagin, "The Pleasures of Tragedy," 95.

13. Alex Neill, "Yanal and Others on Hume on Tragedy," *Journal of Aesthetics and Art Criticism* 50 (1992): 152. Quotes are as cited by Neill.

14. Ibid.

which the mind finds "naturally delightful." And in none of this is there the clear affirmation that the pain of our sorrow over the tragic events or indeed that any other singular, nonpleasurable aspect of our experience is converted into pleasure: Hume's conversion litany says over and over that our *overall* experience of tragedy takes on a pleasurable aspect.

Neill extracts from Hume's essay two cases that he says "illustrate what Hume has in mind in his talk of the 'conversion' . . . of passion."[15] "Parents," Hume says, "commonly love that child most, whose sickly, infirm frame . . . has occasioned them the greatest pains, trouble, and anxiety, in rearing him. The agreeable sentiment of affection here acquires force from sentiments of uneasiness."[16] The case bears on the paradox of tragedy by analogy: the parent's "agreeable sentiment of affection" for their child is like the pleasure we take in tragedy, and the (presumably disagreeable) "sentiments of uneasiness" they felt for him are like the painful emotions we experience in tragedy. This is about all Hume gives us. We are not told how the sentiments operate together, except that the sentiments of affection "acquire force" from the sentiments of uneasiness. The question, then, is how we are to understand the phrase "acquires force." If "love acquires force from uneasiness" means that both emotions operate simultaneously, uniting into an overall experience that is more powerful than it would be without any uneasiness, then we have an example of addition, not conversion, which parallels my interpretation of Hume. Or I should say it parallels it to a point, for love acquiring force is not prima facie a case of something's taking on pleasure. If, on the other hand, we allow that the love itself has been infused with a history of uneasiness (which is the reading Neill prefers), then we have an example in which one passion alters—converts—another. Yet there is no straightforward mapping of this onto the paradox of tragedy. For I do not see what it means to say that the pleasure we take in tragedy is converted by the painful emotions we have experienced, except to say the pleasure we take in tragedy is tinged with pain, which is but a brief restatement of the solution I attribute to Hume.

The other case of conversion Neill offers is a remark about jealousy, which Hume tells us "is a painful passion; yet without some share of it, the agreeable affection of love has difficulty to subsist in its full force and violence."[17] Neill comments that Hume meant that "jealousy and love may become part of each other . . . they may 'mingle and unite' . . . so that the love acquires a jealous character or the jealousy a loving one."[18] I don't know if Hume has said enough to sanction Neill's reading, for Hume has only said something about the "full force and violence" of love—that love achieves its full force and violence [!] only when at the time we love we are also jealous—which does not in itself imply that jealousy joins or transforms or converts or infuses the love with which it coexists. However, suppose for the sake of argument that jealousy converts love. I'm in love with X who, I discover, has been sleeping with Y. I stay in love with X though I become intensely jealous. For the sake of argument we agree that my love has changed: love *simpliciter* has become converted to jealous-love, a more forceful and violent variation of what I had until my discovery felt toward X.[19]

What does this tell us about conversion, tragedy, pleasure, pain, and emotions? Not much, I think. For one thing, the jealousy case does not clearly stand as an example of taking pleasure in pain. That jealousy imparts force and violence to love need not mean that the loving-though-jealous person takes pleasure in his jealousy. He may well wish his jealousy would go away, that he could go back to a less forceful and violent (and more pleasant) love. For another, while it's true that the jealous person continues to love (and arguably, though not indisputably, continues thereby to take pleasure), he might do it *despite*, not because of, the pain of his jealousy. Hume, remember, offers jealousy only as a necessary condition of continuing to love at a certain level of "force and violence" (a remark which I find nearly empty, for there is no noncircular way of identifying this "level" of love, except as a love maintained by jealousy). For a third, while there may be something like conversion going on in the jealousy case, it is not the kind of conversion we were looking for. For what would it mean for the pleasurable sentiment of beauty to "modify" or "mingle with" the unpleasant passion of sorrow? If this turns out to mean that we end up feeling beautiful sorrow, or feeling sorrow beautifully,

---

17. Ibid.

18. Neill, "Yanal and Others on Hume," 154.

19. Hume has a remark on love in the *Treatise of Human Nature* some twenty years before the essay on tragedy: "'Tis altogether impossible to give any definition of the passions of *love* and *hatred*, and that because they produce merely a single impression, without any mixture or composition" (David Hume, *A Treatise of Human Nature* (1739), ed. L. A. Selby-Bigge [London: Oxford University Press, 1964], book 2, part 2, section 1, p. 329). It is natural to conclude that were Hume to be held to this view in the essay on tragedy he could not admit a "mixture" of jealousy into love.

then I'm afraid this is too cryptic to be a solution to anything—and would bring us full circle to those original commentators (Susan Feagin and Mark Packer) who charged Hume with failing to explain the mechanics of how unpleasantness is transformed into pleasantness, a charge from which my combinatory interpretation was supposed to rescue Hume.

Thoughts From Theory T

The general form of a combinatory solution to the tragic paradox is to analyze the overall experience of a narrative that aroused negative emotions into unpleasant elements (the pain of our passions) and pleasant elements (including the aesthetic qualities Hume mentions, and possibly also the meta-responses of satisfaction and pleasures of learning suggested by Feagin, Walton, and Carroll). When the pleasant elements outweigh the painful passions there is enjoyment on the whole. Such a solution is, I'm convinced, on the right path, especially since it does not deny that our experience of tragedy or horror contains painful elements that are not converted or effaced.

Is such a combinatory solution complete, then, as it stands? Hume says that the audience to Cicero's oration on the butchery of the Sicilian captains enjoyed the speech though it raised anger and horror at the injustice, even as they were convinced that the butchery was a real event. But surely the audience would not have enjoyed the actual butchery, though here of course there would be no eloquence to pleasure them. Suppose though that we who enjoy *King Lear* are witness to real events such as are only fictionally represented in Shakespeare's tragedy. But now let the participants of these real-life counterparts of *Lear* put forward many of the aesthetic qualities that ordinarily bring pleasure. These real participants wear beautiful costumes, speak the most beautiful language, use dramatic gestures, and so on, even as they throw old Lear out of their castles, and gouge out Gloucester's eyes. And old Lear himself is sublimely poetic during his madness, and eminently eloquent as he cradles the dead Cordelia.

Will our experience as witness to the real-life *Lear* be overall enjoyable? Surely not, but this means that the combinatory solution advanced is incomplete. We can supplement it with these thoughts from Thought Theory T.

1. Theory T maintains that our emotions are aroused from entertaining in thought the words, images, and sounds projected by the fictional narrative, along with any inferences we may draw. It is our focused involvement with such strings of thoughts that engender any emotion we feel toward fictions. Theory T insists that our belief in the fictionality of the characters be inactivated though not relinquished: the belief should be active enough so as to allow us to maintain, as we might say, our grip on reality.

The belief in fictionality, slightly active, is at work while we view Shakespeare's *King Lear*, but there is no belief in fictionality when we are horrified witnesses to a real-life analogue of this play. When we fully believe that what we are witnessing is real, our pity, sorrow, horror, and any other negative emotions that come into play have no background belief in fictionality to ameliorate them. Hence, even if a real eye gouging is done beautifully and with eloquent speeches, our emotions thereby aroused will be, I suggest, far too painful to be overcome by aesthetic pleasure (if even we bother to attend to aesthetic pleasure during a murder). Aesthetic pleasure can combine with negative emotion to yield an overall pleasurable experience only when the negative emotions are themselves not too painful.

2. Real-life people and events imply a past and future. Fictional representations rarely do. The thoughts we entertain about fictions are largely in the (fictional) here-and-now. Thus a tragic event in real-life has to us ramifications that a fictional tragedy might not. Being witness to a real-life Lear as he cradles the dead Cordelia might call to mind the proud and strong young man Lear was, or the dismal future he now faces, though such implications might not come to us while we entertain thoughts of Lear as delivered by Shakespeare's play. It may be that this broadening of emotional scope with real-life events occasions more painful negative emotions than the more narrowly focused thoughts that fictional representations occasion.

3. Fictions are presented with a certain point-of-view; real-life events are not. Old age can be presented comically (as in Robert Zemeckis's black comedy, *Death Becomes Her*), tragically (as in Hemingway's *Old Man and the Sea*), or matter-of-factly (as in Iris Murdoch's *The Sea, The Sea*). The thoughts we entertain are infected with the point-of-view of the fictional narrative, and point-of-view can ameliorate unpleasantness in a way that real life, which lacks point-of-view, cannot.

summary

The argument has been long and complicated, and perhaps this is a reason to repeat its essentials. The paradox of emotion and fiction arises because we do not believe in the real existence of fictional characters, yet we respond to them as if they really existed. We pity Anna Karenina though we know there is no one suffering what she is said to suffer. A host of explanations of this phenomenon have been offered: we are being irrational; we don't, appearances aside, pity Anna Karenina but pity some actuality that Tolstoy's novel implies; we are playing a game of make-believe and our pity isn't real pity. Yet each of these explanations accepts the necessity of belief for emotion.

Belief, however, is not necessary for emotion. We can feel anxious because we suspect (though not believe) we are late for an important meeting. The thought that we might tumble over a cliff near which we stand can precipitate fear, though we don't believe that we will tumble over that cliff. Such examples suggest that it is the thought that counts, that is, the mere entertaining of thoughts is often sufficient to induce emotion. When we read a novel or view a film we are inspired to thoughts not believed true—for example, the thought that Anna Karenina is suicidal—and such thoughts even in the absence of belief can inspire pity. Several conditions must however be met, the most prominent of which is that our disbelief in the fictional character's real existence must be rendered relatively inactive (though not "suspended" entirely). This is the gist of the thought theory defended earlier. Thought theory T preserves the intuitions that we are not irrational when responding emotionally to fiction and that it is the fictional character not some analogous reality that is the object of our emotion. It also avoids the unnecessary complexities of role-playing and accepts the full reality of emotion toward fiction.

The most useful tenet of thought theory as defended here is its proposed inactivation of disbelief. But if disbelief can be inactivated perhaps other cognitive states can be too. One could, for example, inactivate one's recollection of what comes next, thereby enabling oneself to re-view works and re-experience suspense over and over. Such inactivation seems, however, especially difficult, as one event in a narrative one knows well often triggers the memory of what happens next (seeing King Kong chained on stage enervated by flashing camera almost surely triggers the recollection that he breaks loose from his chains), whereas fictional characters don't constantly tip us off as to their fictionality. Also if we activate our belief in the fictionality of a fictional character, we stand to forfeit the emotional experience of the work; while if we activate our recollection of what comes next in a narrative we know well, we still have other enjoyments including emotional experiences. An experience of a narrative when what comes next is actively recollected need not be impoverished, and may well offer more than the satisfactions accruing to a first-timer.

The inactivation of disbelief may play a role in explaining our enjoyment of works that arouse such painful emotions as pity and fear. The general solution to the puzzle such works arouse is that the pain of the emotions is counterbalanced by aesthetic and other pleasures. Yet actual events that parallel the fictional events of Shakespeare's *King Lear* might arouse emotions that would be too painful to be counterbalanced. The suggestion made by thought theory is that our disbelief in the reality of King Lear, Cordelia, and the others, is inactive but not entirely dormant, and thus may work in the background to modify the pain we feel on viewing Shakespeare's tragedy so that its aesthetic effects can add up to an experience enjoyable overall.

index